DISCARD

THE TRIUMPH
OF SUBJECTIVITY

THE TRIUMPH OF SUBJECTIVITY

AN INTRODUCTION TO TRANSCENDENTAL PHENOMENOLOGY

Quentin Lauer, s.j.

NEW YORK
FORDHAM UNIVERSITY PRESS
1978

Printed in the United States of America

CONTENTS

FOREWORD

To AN OBSERVER of the contemporary intellectual scene, it may appear that the years following the end of the war have witnessed a triumph of phenomenology on an international scale. Certainly, this impression is correct to some extent. Much, however, of what passes for "phenomenology" can thus be taken only in a very broad, not to say extremely loose, sense. Some of the writings about Husserl's phenomenology are too much colored and determined by views current in contemporary philosophical trends which, though they have undoubtedly developed in the wake of Husserl's phenomenology, can not yet be considered as its continuations; that is, as continuations of Husserl's work along the lines of his general orientation. Needless to say, thus to continue Husserl's work is not only compatible with, but might even sometimes demand modifications of, particular theories.

As far as the situation in the United States is concerned, the unfortunate fact of the matter is that Husserl's writings are hardly studied at all, and his theories and ideas remain largely unknown. So by-passed, phenomenology is not permitted to exert the invigorating influence it might have upon contemporary American philosophy which thus deprives itself of the vitalization it might derive from the philosophical substance and radicalism of Husserl's work. No less deplorable are the misconceptions current in what may be called philosophical public opinion: the misunderstanding of Husserl's notion of "intuition" for a kind of mystical insight or illumination; the misinterpretation of his descriptive analyses as a sort of introspectionism, and the like. To be sure, there are some American publications of more or less recent date which do not seem to bear out this pessimistic view. We gratefully acknowledge those encouraging signs and we may even take them as a promise for the future. Yet, at the present phase, they can hardly be considered as more than exceptional and marginal phenomena. It still remains true that phenomenology plays no role in contemporary American philosophy.

Under these circumstances, reliable monographs either on Husserl's phenomenology as a whole or on certain of its central aspects are highly desirable. It is most gratifying to us to welcome and to introduce Quentin Lauer's book. Among the American publications just referred to as hopeful and promising symptoms of a serious interest in and genuine understanding of Husserl's phenomenology, the present book will hold a prominent place.

Husserl's phenomenology is presented by Father Lauer under a genetic perspective. He pursues its gradual unfolding and crystallization through four of Husserl's major works which had appeared during his lifetime; the first in 1900–1901, the last in 1931. For its internal unity and coherence, a presentation which lays bare the growth of phenomenological philosophy requires to be organized around a central theme. For that central theme, Father Lauer has chosen the notion of the intentionality of consciousness.

A more fortunate and appropriate choice could hardly have been made. Not only is the theory of intentionality of predominant importance for Husserl's thought, but one might even go as far as maintaining that a completely developed phenomenological philosophy would coincide with a theory of intentionality, consistently elaborated in all its ramifications. By this insistence upon the presentational function of acts of consciousness — that is, upon their function of confronting the experiencing subject with objects as meant, intended, and appearing through those acts — Husserl has inaugurated a radical change in the current conceptions concerning consciousness and the nature of the mind. Husserl foresaw that the theory of intentionality and phenomenological philosophy as a whole implied drastic reforms of psychological thinking. Trends of contemporary psychology and psychopathology on the continent of Europe bear out this prediction, although not all the authors are always aware of the full measure of their indebtedness to Husserl's notion of intentionality. Philosophically speaking, the theory of the intentionality of consciousness entails a complete renewal and reformulation of the problem of knowledge in its full scope, especially of the problem concerning the relationship between "subject" and "object," a problem whose discussion in traditional terms has long since ended in a blind alley. Along with a new conception of the nature of the mind, there goes a no less radical revision of the notions of "object" and "objectivity."

THE TRIUMPH OF SUBJECTIVITY is most timely at the present moment when American philosophy is overwhelmingly dominated by the several varieties of what is called "analytical philosophy." Nobody will deny that "analytical" philosophy is imbued by the spirit of intellectual responsibility: insistence upon rigor and exactness. There can be no doubt as to what we might call its "intellectual morality," as far as its intentions are concerned. However, the question arises as to how such aims can be attained. Does rigor in philosophical matters depend primarily upon clarity of expression? Can it be attained by defining, re-defining, and repeatedly amending terms, expressions, and formulations? Many discussions in "analytical philosophy" of all varieties are reminiscent of the procedures of lawyers who, with unquestionable competence and great skill, argue their cases, but in so doing remain within a framework which they accept and which does not become questionable to them. To be sure, the very nature of his function fully justifies the lawyer in proceeding as he does. The philosopher, however, cannot afford to operate within a framework which he takes for granted. His very function as a philosopher impels him to become aware of the grounds on which he stands, to make explicit his presuppositions — even if they seem a matter of course — and to pursue these presuppositions to their very roots. Methods of formalization and axiomatization have been most successfully used in some sciences and have yielded most remarkable theoretical results. One can understand the temptation to generalize these methods, to employ them in all fields, including that of philosophy. Relying on their success in certain fields, may one not expect from them similarly successful results in all fields? Yet the question must be raised — why the methods of formalization have proved so successful in certain fields and wherein the very nature of their success consists? One is thus led to inquire into the sense and meaning of those methods, into the presuppositions (of perhaps a most complicated nature) which are involved in their elaboration and their use. It seems obvious that those problems cannot be approached by means of the very methods whose meaning and foundations are in question. Formalization, axiomatization, any method or methodological procedure, whether scientific or pre-scientific, is a mental accomplishment, the outcome of mental operations. Clarification in these matters, therefore, requires a general conception, if not a theory, of consciousness and the mind.

As far as the demands of rigor in philosophical matters are concerned, the standards which Husserl has set and to which he has adhered are hardly matched in any other trend of contemporary philosophy. We dare say that in this respect philosophers can learn a great deal from him. First of all, they can learn that philosophical rigor does not consist in the unquestioned and unexamined acceptance of preconceived models of rigor, whatever prestige has accrued to those models on account of their successful use in other, viz. non-philosophical, fields. Both the refusal simply to emulate "Scientific Method" (written with capital letters) and the insistence upon accounting for the theoretical success of certain methods, whenever legitimately used, seem to us an expression of the true and radical scientific spirit in philosophy.

Father Lauer's book conveys an impression of this scientific spirit, in a radical sense, which was alive in Husserl. He has rendered a valuable service to both the cause of phenomenology and American philosophy. May he find his reward in seeing his book stimulate studies of Husserl's thought at its sources.

Brandeis University   ARON GURWITSCH

x

PREFACE TO THE SECOND EDITION

THE QUESTION may very well be asked: why a new edition of a book on Husserl's transcendental phenomenology twenty years after the original edition was published, twenty years during which Husserl scholarship in English has progressed so far that an elementary text of this kind might now be deemed superfluous? Are the reasons for having published the book in 1958 still valid? The new material and revisions included in the present edition are, in fact, not enormous: a new Preface has been added; the final chapter of the first edition, which had become anachronistic, has been removed; two Appendices have been added; and the material contained in Chapters 1 through 8 has been updated and corrected.

There are two answers to the question, the first rather simple and unsubtle, the second more complex and subtle. The first answer is that the publishers are convinced that there is still room for a relatively simple introduction to Husserl's thought, a book which over these twenty years has had considerable success in helping both teachers and students to enter into the complexities of Husserlian thought and vocabulary, thus smoothing the way to a better comprehension of one of the most important movements in contemporary philosophy, the phenomenological movement. The second answer is that the very proliferation of specialized studies of phenomenological philosophy has made even more imperative a simple orientation in the method developed over a period of forty years by Edmund Husserl and employed with greater or lesser fidelity by a community of scholars who draw much of their inspiration from his efforts.

That the situation for English-speaking readers has changed considerably since this book was first published is unquestionable. In 1958 there existed only two English translations of Husserl's works

— both relatively unreliable. There was the 1931 Boyce-Gibson translation of *Ideen I* (*Ideen II* and *III* were at the time not available even in German). In addition, there was the *Encyclopaedia Britannica* (14th ed.) article "Phenomenology," a severely truncated version of the original German written by Husserl (with the assistance of Eugen Fink). In 1960, Dorion Cairns' translation of *Cartesian Meditations* began an important series of contributions. 1964 saw the publication of James S. Churchill's translation of *Phenomenology of Internal Time Consciousness*, and in 1965 appeared my translation of *Philosophy as Rigorous Science* and *Philosophy and the Crisis of European Man*. Then, in rapid succession (1969–1973) four major works of Husserl appeared in translation: 1969, *Formal and Transcendental Logic*, translated by Dorion Cairns; 1970, *Crisis of European Sciences and Transcendental Phenomenology*, translated by David Carr; 1970, *Logical Investigations* (2 vols.), translated by John Findlay; 1973, *Experience and Judgment*, translated by Churchill and Ameriks. Much, admittedly, still needs to be done both by way of translation and by way of explication of translations which are extremely difficult to read.

To attempt simply to enumerate the books which have appeared in the last twenty years concerned either with Husserl's phenomenology or with the phenomenological endeavor in general would be to engage in an enormous bibliographical enterprise. Suffice it to say that a visit to any university library today would reveal at least two shelves of books, all written between 1970 and the present, on Husserl's phenomenology alone. It is true, of course, that not every one of these books would meet with Husserl's approval; but they are at least a testimony to an impetus he gave to a penetration of reality — and of its *meaning* — which is unique in the history of philosophical investigation. No one, not even Hegel, was more dedicated than Husserl to the proposition that all philosophical investigation is scientific investigation and that all philosophic utterances must be apodictically verified, or else they are simply not philosophical at all.

Philosophy as Rigorous Science, an essay appearing in 1911, is an early indication of Husserl's definitive attitude toward the very nature of philosophical thinking. He was at that time convinced —

and he continued to be throughout his career — that philosophy had to be the ultimate foundation for all knowing and that, for it to be thus foundational, philosophy itself had to be rigorously scientific in its procedures. The basic presupposition, we might say, of Husserl's "presuppositionless" attitude was that nothing short of a strictly scientific philosophy would do. To put it rather bluntly: Husserl's demand was "I want to know, and I want to be sure that what I am doing is *knowing*, not *opining* or *believing*." It is easy to see how near and yet how far Husserl was from Plato's ideal of philosophizing: near, in his insistence on knowledge as opposed to opinion; far, in his antecedent eidetic intuition of the very essence of science, in which the certainty of the knowing was to be more important than the significance of what is known. It was this ideal of Husserl's which dictated the method he *employed* in his earliest writings, a method which he sought to elaborate throughout the rest of his career. Scientific rigor had to be achieved at all costs; this was the "foundational" thinking he sought to accomplish, and this he could accomplish only if philosophy was purely theoretical and only if philosophy's objects were purely ideal. The pursuit of this goal demanded of Husserl an incredible asceticism, which he was willing to undertake because he saw in scientific rigor an indispensable value, for which there simply was no substitute.

It was the vision of this goal which colored Husserl's view of the whole orientation of Western philosophy's history. From its inception Western philosophy had been tending toward the realization of its own scientific essence, and in Husserl's own day Western man was coming to the realization that no other goal was worthy of him. The dominant ideal, then, in all of Husserl's thinking was that of making philosophy scientific. Ultimately this was to mean laying the foundation for *all* scientific thinking by determining the conditions under which the concepts in which scientific knowledge is grasped and expressed are apodictically certain concepts, which cannot (logically) be otherwise for anyone. All of us, we might say, employ concepts, but, says Husserl, we cannot be justified in employing them until we are certain of what is absolutely essential to them.

Only a philosophy, then, which is truly scientific can truly be philosophy — modern man can be satisfied with no less — and only a phenomenology which penetrates to the very essence of the objects the human mind knows can be truly scientific. Husserl's concern is the *quality* of human knowing, and the quality he looks for is apodictic certainty, wherein there is no possibility of error or doubt. The question of certainty, however, very quickly becomes the question of evidence, which is to say, the quality of givenness of the objects which the human mind knows. It is here that, for Husserl, the question of *reason* comes in. The only knowing worthy of the name is rational knowing, and the only rational knowing worthy of the name is that which is grounded in philosophical reason, which has its own discoverable rules which guarantee the logical necessity both of its functioning and of its objects. The transcendental phenomenological method, then, is the method of thinking which assures Husserl that his thinking is authentically rational and, hence, necessarily true. It is in transcendental phenomenology that human reason comes to itself and is, thus, saved. Phenomenology is "transcendental" both in the Kantian sense of a thinking activity which is not simply receptive of an activity stemming from a "transcendent" reality and in the further sense that it embraces all human thinking, thus transcending the thinking of any individual or of any group of individuals.

Although it is true to say that, for Husserl, the subject matter of philosophy dictates the phenomenological method, it would be a mistake to see in this an indication that he is advocating a philosophical system. Husserl was a systematic thinker but anything but an advocate of system. What he called for was a unified method of approach to each philosophical problem in order to clarify and validate significant concepts, but this did not mean the interweaving of concepts into one systematic whole. Quite the contrary: it meant employing the same method over and over again, beginning anew with each distinct problem. Each philosophical conclusion could stand by itself, because each conclusion was to be thoroughly verified through a validation of the concepts it involved. This meant, however, that the truth of his conclusions was to be not *inferred* but *seen*, which is to say that the essential knowledge he sought was intuitive; the method leading up to the intuition was logical, but the intuition itself was a seeing. Only thus, he was convinced, could that which cannot not be (essence) be grasped, and only thus can the knower know that what he knows cannot not be. All of this is to be understood in a framework in which, although the only access to reality we have is through experience, we can validate the experience itself only by employing concepts which are not derived from experience, precisely because the only being which concepts, and thus essences, have is ideal being. If, then, there is no knowing at all without the knowing of essences, it follows both that what is known is ideal, in no sense physical, and that the knowing is ideal, in no sense psycho-physical.

It would be a mistake, however, to conclude that Husserl impugns the validity of the empirical sciences, be they physical or psycho-physical. His very intuition of the essence of science is based on his phenomenological investigation of the sciences which, he was convinced, were already established as sciences antecedently to the establishment of philosophy as a science. What he was seeking, as we said, was foundational thinking, a thinking which would ground the scientificity even of the established sciences. What the intuition of the essence of science told him was that science bespeaks not uniformity of method but only uniformly certain results, which could be guaranteed only if the foundational concepts with which philosophy is concerned have been apodictically verified. This means, in the final analysis, that the certainty of any scientific thinking has been impugned if its ultimate foundations — philosophical concepts — have not been apodictically validated, which they can be only in immediate essential intuitions. What Husserl sought from the beginning, then, was "pure theory" — the very essence of theory — the uniquely true theory (against which the factual diversity of theories does not militate), the theory which would guarantee that scientific concepts are authentically scientific. What Husserl ultimately found — and devoted the last twenty-five years of his career to elaborating — was transcendental subjectivity, the concrete guarantee of rationality both of thought and of the object of thought. Here again, "transcendental" has the double meaning of being the active source of its own objectivity and of transcending any and all individual subjectivities; "transcendental subjectivity" is pure subjectivity as such.

Science, as Husserl conceived it, is possible only if the human mind can in fact intuit the essences of the objects it conceives. The human mind, in turn, can do this only if the essences it seeks are available to it in the experiences it has. It is Husserl's contention that these essences are given in the experiences had of reality — whether that reality be physical things, events, institutions, mathematical concepts, scientific formulae, or logical categories — and that phenomenological investigation has the capacity to make reality give up the secrets it contains, precisely because by validating the experiences, phenomenology can determine exactly what the objects of those experiences are. It is phenomenology which provides the method for investigating experience and of so rationalizing it that its object must necessarily be what rational experience takes it to be. The world of fact, the world we experience, is of course contingent, and so is every fact in that world. It is a world at all, however, only if the essences of what it contains are not contingent, and knowledge of the world is truly knowledge only if these essences, without contingency, are discoverable by the human mind at work. This is not to say that a knowledge of essence is *derived from* experience: rather it is to say that essences can be *seen in* experience, in what appears to the mind when it experiences, and this is true because by using Husserl's method the mind can both eliminate the contingent and plumb the depths of the necessary which is left behind. To take but a very simple — perhaps crude — example: it is contingent that there be a book before me on my desk, and it is contingent that the book before me be red in color or that it be oblong in shape; it is not contingent that red be *what* red is, or that oblong be *what* oblong is, and it is in the experience of the red and the oblong that the essence of each is discovered — red and oblong can be made to *give* themselves as they *essentially* are. The point, however, is not that the human mind can come up with the essence of red or oblong but that it can and must come up with an apodictic grasp of the essence of any of the concepts it employs. If, for example, one can distinguish a community from

xvi

a society with the same precision as one can distinguish color from shape, or the color red from the color green, an intuition of essence has been achieved. Husserl was wedded to the position that only an apodictic grasp of essences merits at all the title of knowledge (in the fullest sense), and that only a grasp which has effectively eliminated all contingent elements in our affirmations can be apodictic. Phenomenology, then, is the "science of science," since it alone investigates what all other sciences either take for granted or ignore — the very essence of their own objects.

That this should be Husserl's position stems from his own eidetic intuition (before elaborating a methodology of eidetic intuition) of the essence of science as theoretical, i.e., oriented to the *what* of what is. Science in this sense, however, makes no sense if there are no objective essences, and objective essences, in turn, make no sense unless consciousness and ideas have a being of their own, a being which has nothing in common with the "real" being of the physical (object) or the psycho-physical (subject). Only from ideal being is it possible to eliminate the last vestiges of contingency and thus arrive at essential necessity. It has often been remarked that Husserl had at best a meager and inaccurate grasp of the history of thought. Whether or not this is true, Husserl was quite correct in seeing that, unless thought and the object of thought have a being which is simply other than physical, it makes no sense at all to speak of a history of thought. His main concern, however, is not the history of thought; it is to make available for investigation the transcendental subjectivity (subjectivity as such), as the only possible source of the kind of being proper to consciousness and ideas. He agrees with Kant that the universality and necessity of acts of cognition function as the guarantee of their objective validity. This means that an act of cognition contains within itself the guarantee of its objective validity and that the philosopher can see the validity of the act by examining the act itself, with no appeal whatever to what is outside the act. To the investigator who knows how to investigate, the act itself reveals its own validity or invalidity, based on the necessary a-priori rules for valid thinking, and the rules themselves are discovered in a minute investigation of transcendental subjectivity, the only conceivable foundation for rational knowledge based on apodictic evidence. It is transcendental subjectivity properly understood which reveals the criteria for determining when an act of consciousness is truly one of *knowing*. The "pure theory" he had sought has been found — in an analysis of transcendental subjectivity. This, of course, will make no sense, unless the objectivities which scientific knowing claims to know with apodictic certainty are themselves intentionally constituted in transcendental subjectivity; the objectivities thus constituted will make sense only if they are essential; and the objectivities will be essential only if their constitution is thoroughgoingly rational — a rationality which can be guaranteed only by the phenomenological method. This, it would seem, explains the paradox of Husserl's claim that his philosophizing was more radically new than any philosophy ever had been, precisely because it was more thoroughgoingly subjective (and, for that reason, more objective!) than any other philosophy had ever dared to be. It is clear, of course, that here we have neither the subjectivity nor the objectivity of Hegel's Spirit. But it is clear also that the subjectivity of the transcendental subject is a far cry from the arbitrariness of individual subjectivity — from "subjectivism," we might say — and in this Hegel and Husserl are at one.

It is Husserl's claim, then, that his is the only philosophy of subjectivity which has ever been truly radical (apart from the fact that Husserl did not know Kierkegaard, he would have found the latter's subjectivity far too "unscientific" for his taste). Such a philosophy would be more thoroughly "transcendental" even than Kant's, because the a-priori laws of objectivity discoverable in transcendental subjectivity would cover far more than the formal aspects of objectivity. For Husserl, the true being of an object — any object — is the being it has in the truly rational consciousness had of it. This is not to assert that this is the only being (*Bewusst-sein*) an object *has*; simply that it is the only being which *counts*, if one is determined to be scientific. It is for this reason that Husserl constantly insists on the need to repeat the reduction to subjectivity. The mind's "natural" tendency, to which there is no once-and-for-all solution, to posit a *Sein* other than *Bewusst-sein* must constantly be resisted; it must be put aside each time the philosopher turns to authentically philosophical investigation.

The result of all this, then, is a complete re-constitution of all philosophical thinking. It may have been that Plato was quite correct in his insistence on ἐπιστήμη in preference to δόξα; it is only with the kind of validation which Husserl's method made possible that the insistence could ever bear fruit! No philosophical affirmation could ever be apodictically verified prior to the assurance that its object has been intentionally constituted in the immanence of consciousness functioning as reason. Two thinkers, e.g., Plato and Husserl, could conceivably make the same affirmation regarding, say, the essence of virtue: the former would make the affirmation naïvely; only the latter could make it philosophically, i.e., scientifically. To be thus scientific the fundamental necessity would be that of adopting the proper attitude.

Of itself, of course, an attitude is not particularly productive. One can adopt as an attitude the determination to accept nothing as (philosophically) true which has not been verified on the basis of incontrovertible (apodictic) evidence and at the same time have at one's disposal no method of incontrovertibly verifying anything whatsoever. It is precisely here that Husserl issues his manifesto of confidence in his own method, the phenomenological method. In one important sense Husserl always remained a thoroughgoing Cartesian — for him the method was the message. There could be no scientific philosophical advance without the phenomenological method — there is simply no other — and the method is to be applied to the investigation of each and every issue to which the philosopher turns his attention. Husserl never expressed any doubt whatsoever that this is *the* method — without it there is no certainty, and certainty is paramount. Philosophy, it is true, is one, but its unity is not the unity of one body of knowledge, all the elements of which are systematically interconnected. Rather it is the unity of one method applied systematically in every investigation.

Here it is that we can see how wide is the gap which separates not only the philosophies but also the methods of Hegel and Husserl. For Hegel the method — dictated by the subject matter — is one of pro-

gressive explicitation of the implications contained in an initial indubitable grasp of the object of consciousness, accomplished through
a progressive negation of satisfaction with any stage in the process
prior to absolute knowing. For Husserl it is a question of establishing
an intuitive critique of the a-priori conditions for the very being of
absolute knowing, methodically eliminating whatever would be an
obstacle to that, and determining precisely what is the apodictically
evident residue of objectivity which survives the process of elimination. Both Hegel and Husserl are convinced that, short of absolute
knowing, there is no guarantee of any knowing, and each is convinced that the method he employs guarantees the absoluteness of
the knowing — for the former it is the dialectical method, for the
latter the transcendental phenomenological method. For both, what
is *known* absolutely *is* absolutely, and for both this is the object of
absolute self-knowing, because what such a knowing knows is.

Our concern here, however, is Husserl, not Hegel. Although it is
true that, for Husserl, the ultimate source of all rationality and, therefore, of all objectivity in knowing is transcendental subjectivity, the
knowing of which guarantees the objectivity of whatever is genuinely
known, the main thrust of his method is the objectivity of the known,
and this ultimately means the essential *whatness* of the objects
known. It may very well be that, as Kant would have it, man's
ultimate concerns are God, freedom, and immortality. As Husserl
sees it, these are not the philosopher's ultimate concern — unless, of
course, he can attain to essential knowledge of these. The philosopher's ultimate concern is to know essences, and even this concern
is guided by the determination to affirm only that of which he can
be certain — and only of essences can he be certain. The process of
philosophizing, then, is the process of becoming certain, and this can
be no other than the process of rendering essences "evident," i.e.,
"present-in-themselves" to the philosopher subject. Husserl began
his scholarly career as a mathematician, and, although he never demanded of philosophical knowledge that it have the same exactitude
as does mathematics, he did demand of philosophical thinking that it
have the same scientific *rigor* as does mathematics, and he saw this as
possible, only if philosophy's objects could be to the philosopher

"present-in-themselves" just as immediately as were the objects of mathematics to the mathematician. It is not difficult to see how mathematical reason can eliminate contingency — and therefore uncertainty — from the ideal entities which are its objects. Not only is it characteristic of mathematical entities that their being known with certainty does not demand that they be embodied in factual reality: they resist being so embodied. They are constituted by the mathematical mind as ideal entities. They are essences and only essences; each is exactly what it is, and each is precisely distinguishable from what it is not. Each is, finally, *seen* in itself as what it is and not *inferred* from some other which it is not. By the same token the objects of philosophical knowing are ideal entities — not mathematical but ontological — which have been constituted in philosophical reason which alone is capable of eliminating in them every last vestige of contingency, i.e., embodiment in the factual. They, too, then, are essences and only essences; each of them is exactly what it is and is distinguishable from what it is not. Each is seen in itself as what it is, and is not inferred from what it is not. Finally, just as the drawing or the corporeal embodiment of the mathematical entity can, as Plato has told us, do no more than "remind" us of the "real" entity, so too, Husserl will tell us, the ideal ontological entity of philosophy has being only in being constituted in the philosophical reason which knows it.

Quite obviously this kind of knowing, this kind of apodictically evident ideal entity, cannot spring fully panoplied from the untutored mind, like Minerva from the head of Jove. The mind in which philosophy's ideal objects are constituted must be a mind which develops, a mind which becomes better and better equipped to know, a mind which has been trained to employ consciously the phenomenological method, not of *finding* evidence but of *making* evident. It is of the essence of any and every "pure" act of consciousness that it be intentionally oriented to one object, and to one object only. That one object of consciousness is apodictically given in that one act of consciousness, in such a way that to know the act in all its uniqueness is to know the object in all its essential uniqueness. It is the character of the act — the subjective logical necessity whereby it sees what it sees — which guarantees the givenness of its object.

One might get the impression that, when all is said and done, Husserl has done no more than give us a method of meaning what we mean, of saying what we mean, and of knowing what we mean when we say it. There is, however, much more to it than that — at least in what Husserl intended to give us. What the transcendental phenomenological method aims at doing is to enable us — nay, to force us — to mean what we *have to* mean, if our conceptualization is to be adequately rational, to say with as much accuracy as the subject matter permits just what that meaning necessarily is, and to know with apodictic certainty that what we mean is the essential meaning of the concept we employ. If we intend any object whatever we intuit its meaning. But that is not enough. Intentions can be arbitrary, meanings can be inaccurate, and language can be tricky. We must *learn* to focus our intentions on one object and on one alone — be it only one "type" of object, with all the inevitable imprecision that implies — to verify our meaning by making that one object obey the a-priori laws of rational necessity, to bring consistency into our language by matching it up with our intentions and our meanings.

That not everyone is going to be satisfied with this program should be fairly obvious. The apparent negativity of so many of the techniques Husserl proposes may to many promise only very impoverished results. Much will depend on what one is looking for. To those who, like Husserl, seek certainty in philosophical knowing, to sacrifice the dross of conjecture for the pure gold of essential knowledge will not be too high a price to pay. But, even those who are not willing to go all the way with Husserl — and none of his more prominent followers was — his method of coming to see what is to be seen and his insistence on seeing as the ultimate criterion of what is known can throw new light on the relation of experience and conceptualization. In any event, since thinking cannot appeal to non-thinking for its validation, a method which promises to validate thinking by appealing only to the a-priori conditions of thinking itself bears looking into. If it is true to say that the structure of reality is to be found in the structure of rational thinking — and where else have we to look?

— then a method of determining the structure of rational thinking is not to be ignored. Perhaps what we shall ultimately say is that the ideal of scientific rigor in philosophical thinking leaves us cold — but should we say this without first giving careful attention to the ideal?

THE TRIUMPH
OF SUBJECTIVITY

WHAT IS PHENOMENOLOGY?

WITH THE PASSAGE OF TIME it becomes more and more difficult to determine what the words "phenomenology" and "phenomenological" are supposed to mean in the contexts in which they are used. Like the terms "existentialism" and "existential" it has become fashionable to designate thereby some sort of profound, recondite, and very up-to-date approach to philosophy or science, without its being entirely clear in what sense the terms are being applied. There is a sense, of course, in which this vague use is justified, since every attempt to get away from speculative constructionism and to limit oneself to the data which are presented in consciousness — describing rather than explaining them — is to that extent phenomenological, at least in method. Still, the sort of vagueness which goes with modishness leads to confusion and makes for a terminology almost empty of meaning. In recent years, for example, phenomenology has in some minds become so intimately bound up with existentialism that the two terms are used almost indiscriminately, despite significant differences in the attitudes represented by the two titles. The reason for this may be that the thought of Jean-Paul Sartre, which is both phenomenological and existential, is taken as typical. Many thinkers, such as Martin Heidegger and Gabriel Marcel, who consider their own approach to philosophy as phenomenological, have expressly indicated their desire not to be identified with the direction represented by Sartre. Others, such as Jean Hering or Dietrich von Hildebrand, would see no sense in referring to their thought as in any way "existential."

In whatever context the term phenomenology is used, however, it refers back to the distinction introduced by Kant between the *phenomenon* or appearance of reality in consciousness, and the *noumenon,* or being of reality in itself. Kant himself did not develop a phenomenology as such, but since his *Critique of Pure Reason* recognizes scientific knowledge only of *phenomena* and not at all of *noumena,* his critique can be considered a sort of phenomenology. According to this position whatever is known is phenomenon, precisely because to be known means to appear to consciousness in a special way, so that what does not in any way appear is not known — at least not by speculative reason. Still, according to Kant, it is possible to *think* what is not *known,* and this we think of as a "thing-in-itself" or *noumenon,* of which the *phenomenon* is the known aspect. This sort of phenomenology, which will restrict scientific knowledge to appearances, is directed both against the rationalism of Descartes, which seeks a rational knowledge of all reality, and against the phenomenism of Hume, which will accept no scientific knowledge at all except that of mathematics. Kant insists that there can be true scientific knowledge which is not mathematical, but he denies that there can be such a knowledge in metaphysics.

The first philosopher to characterize his own approach to philosophy as phenomenology was Hegel. Like Kant he contended that phenomena are all we have to go on, but unlike Kant he was convinced that they afforded a sufficient basis for a universal science of being. He saw no need of even thinking of an unknown thing-in-itself. Phenomena, according to Hegel, reveal all that is to be revealed — not simply in themselves but through the medium of the dialectical process, which is the necessary process of human thought. Beginning with the simplest form of consciousness, which is immediate sense perception, he brings us through consciousness of self (in a series of dialectics which reveal the social and historical nature of knowledge) to reason, wherein reality is reduced to unity, ultimately to that of the Absolute Idea, Absolute Spirit, which *is* all reality. To be *fully* conscious of self is to be fully conscious of all reality, since the ultimate self is all reality. In all this Hegel sees no departure from the original phenomenon, since the dialectical process constitutes an unbreakable chain which has never lost contact with the first experience.

2

With the positivism of Ernst Mach and of the Vienna Circle, which drew its inspiration from Mach, we find another kind of phenomenology, which is not ordinarily characterized as such. In spirit these men were closer to Kant than they were to Hegel, since they preferred Kant's rejection of metaphysics (at least from the point of view of speculative reason) to Hegel's affirmation of it. They would ask no questions at all with regard to reality, convinced as they were that to such questions there were no answers; they were simply satisfied with describing consciousness, the data of which are susceptible only of description, not of explanation. And in this description they found no grounds for affirming a reality, whether it be the "substance" of Spinoza or the "thing-in-itself" of Kant. An approach so exclusively descriptive as this is obviously completely non-metaphysical. Unfortunately, however, many particular positivist interpretations have a tendency not only to eliminate reality as an object of scientific inquiry but to reject any reality whatever, a position which in its negative way is just as metaphysical as its opposite. When Freud in his clinical work confines himself to a pure description of the behaviors he has observed, his approach, too, can be called phenomenological, at least to the extent that any description of what is observed will always be phenomenological.[1] It is, of course, problematical just how successful one can be in completely avoiding any metaphysics whatever — unless one confines oneself to a pure analysis of meaning, which is what the logical positivists of the Vienna Circle do. This results in a sort of mathematics of language, which is probably more purely descriptive than even the most completely conscious phenomenology.

When the term "phenomenology" is used today it usually refers to the philosophy of Edmund Husserl or of some one of those who have drawn their inspiration from him. From the beginning of his philosophical career, Husserl was opposed to what he called the "dualism" of Kant, the "constructionism" of Hegel, and the "naturalism" or "psychologism" of the positivists. He agrees with them in asserting that only phenomena are *given,* but he will claim

---

1. Martin Heidegger, *Sein und Zeit* (7th ed.; Tübingen: Niemeyer, 1953), p. 35, says that the expression "descriptive phenomenology" is tautological — the two terms are inseparable.

that *in* them is given the very *essence* of that which is. Here there is no concern with reality as existing, since existence is at best contingent and as such can add to reality nothing which would be the object of scientific knowledge. If one has described phenomena, one has described all that can be described, but in the very constant elements of that description is revealed the *essence* of what is described. Such a description can say nothing regarding the existence of what is described, but the phenomenological "intuition" in which the description terminates tells us *what* its object *necessarily* is. To know this is to have an "essential" and hence a "scientific" knowledge of being. Contemporary phenomenologists usually follow the development elaborated by Husserl — at least in its methodological aspects — though many of them have rejected the idealistic and metaphysical implications of Husserl's own position. They consider as phenomenology's distinctive mark its capacity to reveal essences, not its refusal to come to terms with "existing" reality. Unlike the investigations of Husserl, those of his followers range over a very wide field, so that there is scarcely an aspect of philosophy or of science which has not been investigated phenomenologically. To mention but a few: we find that Heidegger, Jaspers, Sartre, Marcel, and Conrad-Martius are developing the phenomenological method in its ontological implications; Pfänder, Geiger, Merleau-Ponty, Ricoeur, and Binswanger apply it to psychology; Scheler, von Hildebrand, and Hartmann have developed a phenomenological ethics and general theory of values; Otto, Hering, and Van der Leeuw have studied religion in the same way; while in aesthetics Simmel, Ingarden, Malraux, Duffrenne, and Lipps have been conspicuously successful. Among these same authors we find contributions to epistemological, sociological, linguistic, and logical developments. All are in one way or another concerned with the *essences* of the concepts employed in these disciplines.

Though there is a certain unity of purpose discernible in all these efforts, still there is a certain disadvantage in speaking of the phenomenological method or of phenomenology, without further qualification. The disadvantage is twofold. First of all, the genius of Kant has been so influential that one almost inevitably thinks

4

of phenomena in terms of the Kantian dichotomy of *phenomenon* and *noumenon*, thus giving rise to the opinion that a phenomenology must be either a phenomenism *à la* Hume, which simply refuses to go beyond sensible appearances, or else an introductory stage to a sort of noumenology, which would be some kind of modified Scholasticism, wherein the being which is sought would be something "behind" the phenomenon. The second disadvantage is that, even where the distinction between phenomenology and phenomenism is recognized, there is a tendency to group all phenomenologists together, without attention to the really great differences between the phenomenologies of Scheler, Husserl, Marcel, and Heidegger — to mention a few. It is true, of course, that Husserl provided the impetus for what might loosely be termed "the phenomenological movement," but in so doing he evolved a philosophy which is peculiarly his own, in which no one of his disciples followed him to the limit. Still, if we are to understand what phenomenology means as a contemporary philosophical attitude, we must first understand what it meant in the mind of its founder, Edmund Husserl.

* * *

The problem of reconciling reality and thought about reality is as old as philosophy — we might say, as old as thought itself. The problem is complicated by the obvious fact that we cannot know reality independently of consciousness, and we cannot know consciousness independently of reality — to do so would be to meet the one and the other in isolation, which is an impossibility. We meet consciousness only as consciousness of something; and we meet reality only as a reality of which we are conscious. It seems reasonable to assume that the normal individual will, without reflection, see a certain duality in his experiences of the world about him: in them there is a world which he experiences, and which he assumes to be independently of himself pretty much as he experiences it; and there is also the experience wherein he grasps this world, which he assumes to be distinct from the world. It is also reasonable to assume that he has never been able to analyze his experiences to such an extent that he can isolate — the way one does in analyzing water into hydrogen and oxygen (if even that is possible) — the "elements" which belong to the "independent" world of reality and those which have been contributed by the very act of experiencing this reality. Finally, it seems reasonable to assume that he will not be too much concerned.

The philosopher, however, is committed to penetrating this mystery — for mystery it is — and to coming up with some sort of consistent reconciliation of the two worlds, if he is to continue plying his trade. In a certain sense, the history of philosophy is the record of a series of attempts to make this reconciliation. The problem as it faces us, and as it has faced philosophers from the beginning of philosophizing — apart from the accuracy of the original judgment which the "normal" individual makes — offers a limited number of approaches to a solution. One can approach it from the side of the reality of which we are conscious, from that of the consciousness we have of reality, or from the point of view of a contact between the two. Despite the limited number of approaches, however, there seems to be no limit to the explanations which have been and will continue to be attempted.

The phenomenologist is no exception in this almost universal quest for a solution.[2] Whatever may be his particular position, he seeks to reduce the problem to its simplest terms and *in* them, rather than *from* them, to find a solution, or at least, the approach to a solution. According to the phenomenologist, if there is a solution at all, it must be contained in the *data* of the problem — although, of course, there is a disagreement as to what the data are. The point of agreement, however — and this is what makes each a phenomenologist — is that only phenomena are *given* and that therefore, if an answer is to be found, it must be sought in phenomena.

---

2. We say "almost universal" because the positivist *claims*, at least, to be utterly unconcerned with the *what* of reality or of consciousness. His only objection to any "explanation" which may be given should be that he cannot understand what the explanation means, which is fair enough, if he remains there.

There will be a disagreement as to just what are to be considered as phenomena and as to what can be discovered in them, but there will be agreement that we cannot enlist the aid of the non-phenomenal in seeking our solution. As Maurice Merleau-Ponty, one of the most coherent of the phenomenologists, has expressed it, "Phenomenology is an inventory of consciousness as of that wherein a universe resides." [3] If we are to know what anything is — and this the phenomenologist will do — we must examine the consciousness we have of it; if this does not give us an answer, nothing will.

The consciousness with which the phenomenologist is here concerned is not consciousness as a psychic function, in the way it is, for example, to the experimental psychologist. He is concerned with consciousness as a kind of being which things exercise, the only kind of being directly available to the investigator. Thus, for him, consciousness is best expressed by the German word *Bewusstsein,* which means the kind of being an object of knowledge has in being known. This is not necessarily an identification of being and being-known, but it is an assertion that the only key we have to being is in examining its being-known. Now, even a superficial examination of any act of consciousness will reveal two inescapable facts: (1) it cannot be isolated from other acts of consciousness, but belongs to a whole life of consciousness, is conditioned by all the dispositions of which a subject is capable, is prepared for and colored by the whole series of conscious acts which have preceded it; (2) it is never completely arbitrary, in the sense of being conditioned only subjectively; it is what it is because it is consciousness of this or that object, which, precisely as an object, is in some sense independent of the individual act wherein it is grasped; there is some similarity between the experiences of one subject and another when faced with a similar situation, no matter what the previous experiences of the two may have been.

The attempt to reduce the problem to its simplest terms, however, is not so simple after all. If the only approach we have is through

3. *La structure du comportement* (3rd ed.; Paris: Presses Universitaires de France, 1953), p. 215.

consciousness, and if every act of consciousness is a complex of inseparable elements, some objective and some subjective, the analysis of consciousness which will reveal to us the very meaning of being is a complex affair. The phenomenologist, however, is convinced that this analysis can be made and that in making it he can return to the very origin of consciousness, distinguishing what is pure consciousness from all the accretions which custom, prejudice, assumption, and tradition have built around it. When he has uncovered consciousness in this pure form, he is convinced that he will have arrived at an understanding of the only being which can have significance for him.

In speaking thus of phenomenology we have admittedly come to treat exclusively of the kind of phenomenology advocated by Edmund Husserl and by those who follow him more or less closely. In this sense phenomenology is both a method and a philosophy. As a method it outlines the steps which must be taken in order to arrive at the pure phenomenon, wherein is revealed the very essence not only of appearances but also of that which appears.[4] As a philosophy it claims to give necessary, essential knowledge of that which is,[5] since contingent existence cannot change what reason has recognized as the very essence of its object.[6] In the

4. According to Husserl, there is no essence other than that discoverable in appearances.

5. "Phenomenology, which will be nothing less than a theory of essence contained in pure intuition," from *Ideen I*, edited by Walter Biemel on the basis of the author's own marginal notations to the 1922 edition (The Hague: Martinus Nijhoff, 1950), 154. "With regard to phenomenology, it wants to be a *descriptive* theory of essences," *ibid.*, p. 171. Among the followers of Husserl there is considerable divergence of emphasis, some stressing the *description* of phenomena, others stressing the discovery of *essences* in phenomena. As is so frequently the case, the differences seem to be traceable to the predispositions which each has brought with him in his approach to phenomenology.

For a complete Bibliography of significant Husserliana, consult the author's *La phénoménologie de Husserl* (Paris: Presses Universitaires de France, 1954).

6. If there is any difference at all between phenomenon and reality, it cannot be other than accidental, since the essence of that which is remains absolutely identical. "Immanent being, then, is undoubtedly absolute being, in the sense that, in principle, *nulla 're' indiget ad existendum*," *ibid.*, p. 115; cf. *Nachwort zu meinen Ideen* (Halle: Niemeyer, 1930), p. 14.

8

course of its investigations, therefore, it discovers (or claims to discover) that the quasi infinity of objects which go to make up an experienced world can be described in terms of the consciousness wherein they are experienced. Phenomenology is conceived as a return to "things," as opposed to illusions, verbalisms, or mental constructions, precisely because a "thing" *is* the direct object of consciousness in its purified form. The color "red" is no less a thing than is a horse, since each has an "essence" which is entirely independent of any concrete, contingent existence it may have. It is sufficient that the experience of red can be as clearly distinguished from the experience of green as can the experience of horse from that of man. The dispute as to whether colors are "primary" or "secondary" qualities is entirely without significance; each color has an essence which can be grasped in consciousness, precisely because the essence of any color is contained in the experience of that color. The fact that the content of this experience is an essence is manifest from the fact that it can be clearly distinguished from whatever is essentially something else.[7] In this sense an imaginary object has its distinct *essence* just as truly as does a "real" object. Whether an object is *real* or *fictitious* can be determined by an analysis of the act of which it is object.

All this, however, would be without significance if it were not aimed at discovering "objective" essences, which are what they are not only independently of contingent existence but also independently of any arbitrary meaning which a subject *wants* to give them. Though it is of the essence of an object to be related to a subject, the phenomenologist will deny that "things" act upon subjects in such a way as to engender this relation, or that subjects simply "produce" objects. He will insist that by investigating pure consciousness he can discover a relationship which is truly objective, in the sense that

7. Moritz Schlick has objected that phenomenology has labored hard to produce some very inconsequential distinctions, which distinctions are ultimately nothing more than the distinctions one chooses to assign to terms: cf. "Is there a Factual *A Priori?*", *Readings in Philosophical Analysis*, edd. Feigl and Sellars (New York: Appleton-Century-Crofts, 1949), pp. 277–85. There is, it is true, in the works of the phenomenologists a suspicion that the distinctions they make are derived from convictions which antecede the use of the phenomenological method.

its validity is not derived from the conscious act wherein the relationship resides, and is necessary, in the sense that it could not be otherwise, no matter who the subject grasping the object may be. Husserl's own phenomenological investigations were, it is true, chiefly logical, epistemological, and to a certain extent ontological. Still, phenomenology even as he conceived it is at its persuasive best in the realm of values.

Realistic systems of philosophy have always found the question of moral, religious, aesthetic, and social values a particularly difficult hurdle to clear since the subjective elements in all value judgments are too obvious to be ignored. One can, of course, explain evaluations in terms of the objective values which are being judged, and then describe objective values in terms of their relationship to an evaluating subject; but this sort of thing looks suspiciously like going around in a circle. It is perhaps for this reason that there were no consistent attempts to evolve theories of value, until the days when idealism was enjoying widespread triumph. Idealistic theories, however, have always run the risk of becoming so subjective that the very concept of value loses any communicable significance. Husserl himself was not particularly successful — we might even say that he was eminently unsuccessful — in coming to terms with the complicated problems of value,[8] but his theories, particularly in their ontological aspects, inspired others to look for a world of values which are *what* they are independently of any particular or general judgments regarding them. According to Scheler, Hartmann, von Hildebrand, and others such values are to be *discovered in* things and not to be *imposed on* things by an observing — and evaluating — subject. And the techniques for discovering them are to be the phenomenological techniques of objective analysis and description, resulting in an *"intuition"* of value essences (essential values).

It is not our purpose in this study to examine all (or even some)

8. In a sort of diary, Husserl recounted, in September, 1916, his decision to pursue theoretical truth as a value in preference to other values in life. Neither here nor anywhere else, however, does he justify the objectivity of the value judgment itself. See "Philosophie als strenge Wissenschaft," *Logos,* I (1911), 289–341 at 338.

of the theories which can in one way or another be called phenomenological. It is rather to examine more in detail the theoretical bases for phenomenology as such, as conceived and elaborated by Husserl. From this, it is hoped, we shall be able to understand the ideal which Husserl held out of avoiding in philosophical investigations the Scylla of uncritical objectivism and the Charybdis of arbitrary subjectivism. Husserl himself, it is true, does not seem to have seen, or at least formulated clearly, the possibility of a dialectical interplay of subjective and objective elements in all thought about being, but he did see the necessity of lessening the gap between the subjective and the objective, and even, if necessary, of refusing entirely to recognize its existence. He also faced the necessity of approaching the problem with the only instruments at his disposal, with the instruments clearly contained in consciousness itself. His insistence on remaining completely and purely rational [9] throughout the process made it impossible for him to enjoy fully the riches which his digging had uncovered; but his is still the merit of having uncovered them. [10]

* * *

If we are to understand and appreciate Husserl's lifework, we must see it in terms of the goal he set for himself early in his philosophical career. We say "early in his philosophical career" advisedly, since he began that after many years of work in science and mathematics — not until he was preparing for his doctorate in mathematics at the age of twenty-five did he become interested in philosophy at all. From the first his attitude toward philosophy seems to have been somewhat messianic. Convinced that the highest

9. "This aim or principle of the greatest possible rationality we recognize as the loftiest aim of the rational sciences," *Logische Untersuchungen,* I (4th ed.; Halle: Niemeyer, 1928), 216.

10. Husserl was convinced that the groundwork of this sort of rationality had to be firmly laid before any further advances could be made. For this reason his whole work takes on an extremely programmatic character; he saw his own function as that of assuring the possibility of advancing on solid ground.

ideal represented in the modern age was the scientific ideal and equally convinced that philosophy, as an investigation of the very meaning of being, represented the highest aspiration of the human spirit in any age, he could see no possibility of solution except in an identification of the two ideals. True, he would not seek, with Descartes or Spinoza (as he knew them), to make philosophy scientific in the *way* that mathematics is, but he would insist that in its own way philosophy be *just as* scientific as is mathematics. If it were any less than scientific in the most rigorous sense it would be inferior to mathematics and the positive sciences, which is to say it would not be philosophy, since the term itself signifies the human discipline which is inferior to none.[11]

What Husserl does not seem to have realized is that any judgment as to the relative superiority of science is a value judgment which in this form simply assumes the validity of the value standard it sets. Even less has he re-examined the roots of the judgment wherein he simply identifies philosophy and the highest aspiration of the human spirit.[12] That is equivalent to defining philosophy as that discipline which is superior to any other discipline: whatever that discipline may be it is to be called philosophy. Since there are strict sciences, however, no discipline can be superior to all others if it is not itself a strict science. If we add to this the fact that philosophy has historically been considered the discipline which investigates the very significance of being itself, then Husserl's contention that it is the science of all sciences becomes at least understandable; it is the science which investigates the being which all other sciences simply take for granted. What is less easy to understand, however, is Husserl's contention that philosophy has no right to the name unless it is scientific,[13] and his further contention that since, up to the present,

11. He never, of course, *defines* philosophy in this way, but it is clearly the presupposition upon which is based all he has to say about philosophy.

12. Cf. *Philosophie als strenge Wissenschaft*, pp. 290, 293.

13. Though Husserl does not mention Kant specifically in this connection, this would obviously constitute a rejection of Kant's whole *Critique of Practical Reason* and *Metaphysics of Morals*. This rejection is made specific by Max Scheler in his *Formalismus in der Ethik und die materiale Wertethik* (4th ed.; Bern: Francke, 1954).

no truly scientific philosophy has existed, no philosophy in the strict sense has up to the present existed.

This last contention is important since it explains Husserl's attitude to the history of philosophy. History is significant, for him, because it records a series of abortive attempts to constitute a scientific philosophy, but it is not significant as a progressive development of philosophy itself. Philosophy cannot develop until it exists, and it cannot exist until it is truly scientific, which is to say until it is phenomenological, and this, says Husserl, it has never been.[14] It has, of course, been objected more than once that a discipline whose object is being cannot be a science in the strict sense, precisely because such an object does not admit of strictly scientific verification. Here it is that Husserl, by taking recognized positive sciences and mathematics as examples, seeks to determine what science is essentially,[15] in order thereby to show that an investigation of being can realize this essence, even though in a different way from other sciences. Existence is, admittedly, contingent and therefore not susceptible of being known with the sort of absolute certitude which is characteristic of science. Since, however, it is possible to know what being is independently of existence, a science of being is not only possible but imperative.

That a scientific knowledge of being is imperative might very well be disputed, and has been by many. For Husserl, however, it is obvious: no science can be completely scientific until it knows *what* it is talking about, and no particular science is ever concerned with the *what* of the very concepts it employs most. The mathematician speaks of numbers, dimensions, figures; the physicist speaks of

14. It can well seem amazing that Husserl never recognized the phenomenology of Hegel as meeting this requirement. His disregard of history, however, was based not so much on an extensive examination which convinced him of the inadequacy of previous philosophical positions; rather it is his initial conviction that only a philosophy which is scientific, in the sense in which he understands science, is worthy of consideration at all.

15. In speaking of essence in this way Husserl has taken a page from Kant's book. Strictly speaking the *essence of science* is a limit-idea, which need never be realized but only approached asymptotically. There is an essence of science, even though there never has or will be an adequate realization of the idea.

weight, mass, volume, density; the psychologist, of sensation, cognition, volition — and each arrives at extremely worth-while conclusions. No scientist, however, knows what either his evidence or his conclusions *mean,* unless he knows the *essence* of the objects with which he deals; and no particular science can get at the essence of anything. Only a "science of essences" can do that, and only a phenomenology can be this kind of science, since only a phenomenology can isolate "things" from all the elements of contingency which attach to them in ordinary, "naïve" experience. From beginning to end the work of Husserl is, first of all, an elaboration of the method whereby we can arrive at this sort of *essential* knowledge of things, and secondly, a progressive recognition of the factors which must be taken into consideration if the ideal of complete "verification" of all cognitions is to be realized.

Husserl's philosophical career began in Vienna, in 1884, when, after completing his studies in mathematics, with a minor in philosophy, he attended Franz Brentano's lectures for two years. Brentano's appeal to Husserl can be explained, in part at least, by his attachment to the scientific ideal in philosophy. This ideal was to mean something entirely different for Husserl, who was to remain to the end mathematician and logician in spirit, but it is from these days under Brentano that we can date Husserl's messianic aim of renewing the whole of philosophy by making it strictly scientific.

In the course of a long and prolific life of philosophic reflection there is little evidence that Husserl ever questioned the scientific ideal as such. His attitude throughout seems to have been: philosophy *must* be scientific, if it is to be philosophy; and if it *must,* it *can.* The modern age, which has had a taste of science, will be satisfied with nothing less. It would be a mistake, however, to think that science meant for Husserl what it meant for the positive scientists of his day. Before even elaborating the phenomenological method as a theory he was applying it to the very concept of science. Convinced that he had discovered the very essence of science, which would necessarily be exactly the same wherever there was a true science, despite particular differences which might

14

characterize individual sciences, he set out to realize this essence in philosophy. This meant developing a truly universal science, which would function in each particular science, precisely because it could discover the essences which the individual science presupposed but could not by its own means validate. Particular sciences are concerned with *how* things *act,* but only one science is concerned with *what* things *are;* it is universal because all other sciences can learn from it and only from it *what* their own objects *are.*

Now, it should be obvious that philosophy conceived in this way cannot by any means be a "system." In so far as it is guided by a unity of aim and of method it can be called "systematic," but since it must examine "things" one by one in order to determine their essences, it cannot have the organic unity of a system which grows out of one fundamental principle. Rather, its unity is, as Husserl himself expresses it, the unity of a well-built edifice, wherein one solid stone is placed on another.[16] The knowledge of one essence cannot be derived from the knowledge of another; each must be examined by itself and completely verified in itself.

There is, of course, a disadvantage in this kind of philosophy; the edifice can never be considered complete; it requires the tireless efforts of generations of scholars all imbued with the same conviction, who will discover one by one the essences of those things about which men have been talking since the beginning of time. On the other hand it has the distinct advantage of not being committed to an explanation which must fit in with a preconceived system. Mistakes can be made without endangering the whole edifice; mistakes can be corrected without tearing down the edifice. Nor does one have to wipe the slate clean in order to begin; the investigation of any essence whatever is a beginning; and each investigation is a new beginning. If in a particular science new discoveries are made, the discoveries can be submitted to an essential investigation without the need of revising the whole framework of previous knowledge. According to Husserl, to know an essence is to know that which is necessary and hence eternally true. Knowledge as such cannot be

16. Cf. *Philosophie als strenge Wissenschaft,* pp. 292, 337.

revised, since, by definition, knowledge is necessarily true, and therefore eternally true. It is for this reason that history has so little significance for Husserl; no historical position in philosophy can be accepted until it has been re-examined in the light of the phenomenological method, and once it has been re-examined, it makes no difference that it is an historical position. It is, of course, inconceivable that any individual should work out *all* philosophical problems for himself, but at least in the framework of the scientific community of scholars all problems should be re-examined; for each a return must be made to the fundamental data of the problem, and it must be resolved in essential insights. It may be, of course, that some traditional viewpoints are correct, but they can be accepted only after complete phenomenological verification, since until this verification is complete they represent only opinion and not knowledge.

It would, however, be incorrect to say that Husserl is *completely* unhistorical in his attitude. In his last works, at least, he recognizes two ways in which philosophy can be historical. First, though scientific philosophy and hence philosophy as such has up to his time not existed, there is a history of striving toward the ideal of science recognizable from Plato down to the present day. It is even conceivable that this process was necessary in order that there should ever have been a phenomenological philosophy at all. In this sense the record of generations of striving is a "history" of philosophy. Secondly, since no act of consciousness can be isolated from the "flow" of conscious acts in which it occurs, each act is conditioned by those which precede it. Thus, each experience can be what it is, only because the experiences which have gone before have prepared for it. Since in a broad sense all direct knowledge can be called experience, and since ultimately only direct knowledge can be essential knowledge, there is recognizable a progress in essential knowledge, both on the individual and on the social level, and this progress can be called its history. Since in both cases, however, there can be knowledge strictly speaking only where the phenomenological method is consciously employed, whatever history philosophy as philosophy may have must begin with Husserl himself — that is to say, at least nothing of the past can be considered *essential* to present philosophical thought.

* * *

Though we have already touched on the distinction which Husserl makes between the "exact" science of mathematics and the "strict" science of philosophy, it might be well to terminate this introduction with an examination of the distinction between the essences with which the two kinds of science are concerned. This is particularly important, since only in the light of this distinction can we understand various attempts to realize Husserl's method in areas such as the psychological, the ethical, the sociological, and the aesthetic.

Phenomenology, as we have pointed out, is a study of consciousness. It is not, however, a psychological study of consciousness. Rather, it is an attempt to examine each act of consciousness as a "pure" act of consciousness, seeking to discover in each its essence. Now, in 1900, while writing his *Logical Investigations*, Husserl submitted consciousness itself to a phenomenological investigation. He came to the conclusion that it is the very essence of consciousness to be "consciousness-of" something. Thirty years later, in the *Cartesian Meditations*, which was to be the last of Husserl's major works published during his lifetime, he expressed the same insight by saying that the essence of the Cartesian *cogito* contained the *cogitatum* as immediately as the *cogito* itself. In both expressions Husserl was saying that an act of consciousness and its object are inseparable or, as he said in *Ideas I*, published in 1913, they are but the subjective and objective aspects of the same thing. Thus, to know an act of consciousness adequately, which is to say essentially, is to know its object. What is more, it is to know the object absolutely, in a state of isolation from the contingent conditions of its existence, which is at best always subject to doubt. To know, then, the essence of any conscious act is to know the essence of its object, and that is to have scientific knowledge of its object.

Now, objects of consciousness are many and varied. They may be things or thoughts, persons or events, categories or states of affairs, or they may be mental constructs such as numbers or geometrical figures. Each of these objects has an essence which can be "seen" immediately in an adequate view of the act of consciousness wherein it is contained. The last two, however, differ from all the rest in being entirely products of consciousness itself and therefore not subject to the conditions which progressive experience imposes on all other objects. Mathematical essences are static and changeless; they can be fixed once and for all and described with perfect exactitude. Of other essences it is possible to have strict knowledge, but it must be a knowledge conformed to the types of essence with which it is concerned. Here, too, a distinction must be made. If the object in question is a physical thing it is experienced constantly as identical, which is to say that it has a "nature," which along broad lines at least can be determined with exactitude. Where, however, it is the essence of the phenomenon itself which has to be determined, there is no fixity of nature, there is only the mobility of the vital flow of consciousness, which will cease to be what it is if it is immobilized. Of the phenomenon no exact knowledge is possible, but this is not to say that its essence is not scientifically knowable. If the phenomenon has an essence at all, this essence is scientifically knowable and within somewhat broader limits describable, at least sufficiently to distinguish it from other essences. This is scientific knowledge of essences, since it is knowledge of essences *as they are,* which is to say, as non-fixed, morphological essences, which can be described in terms of "types," though not in terms of exactly determinable "classes."

In all this it may seem that the whole basis of phenomenology has been undermined, since no object can be known except in the appearance whereby it is present to consciousness, which appearance cannot be described with any degree of exactitude. Husserl's point, however, is that it can be described in a manner adequate to the essence in question. To describe this sort of essence *exactly* would be to falsify it, whereas to describe it in the way which the phenomenological method permits is to describe it within limits which are sufficiently narrow to permit that the knowledge based on it be called "scientific."

Instead, then, of undermining the basis of phenomenology, we might say that the modification introduced with the notion of a "morphological" essence has saved it from an impossible situation. Rather than the sort of science which is quite obviously not achievable in philosophy, phenomenology advocates an attempt to understand being in terms of essence, while recognizing that there must be a certain latitude in the conception of *what* essences are. Coupled with a real attempt at intersubjective understanding, the sort of essential insight which Husserl describes might well provide a basis for the dialogue whereby Plato sought to approach the essences of things. Though Husserl himself may have conceived it in a too narrowly scientific sense, it is significant that phenomenology has provided a basis for tendencies as diverse as the personalism of Max Scheler, Martin Heidegger's philosophy of existence, Gabriel Marcel's Christian existentialism, and Maurice Merleau-Ponty's dialectical philosophy of form. In what follows we shall attempt to describe more in detail the principal elements of the phenomenological method, as Husserl understood it, in order thereby to penetrate more deeply into the whole movement he set on foot.

DEVELOPMENT OF A "PURE" PSYCHOLOGY

IN A VERY REAL SENSE the philosophy of Edmund Husserl was revolutionary. It was not revolutionary in the sense that it introduced concepts which were completely new in the history of Western thought. It was, however, revolutionary in the sense that in the era in which it was developed it reintroduced concepts which philosophers had to all intents and purposes already relegated to the realm of the forgotten or perhaps the merely mythical. Perhaps the most important of these concepts and at the same time the most foreign to the ears of his contemporaries was that of *essence*. It was Husserl's intention that philosophy should be precisely a discipline, providing a method and instituting a technique for grasping the very essence of the objects which the human intellect can consider.[1] Positivism and what Husserl called "psychologism" had simply dispensed with any consideration of essences, either because they considered the very concept fantastic or because they thought there was no possibility that the human intellect could grasp what essence was supposed to represent. Husserl, on the contrary, was convinced from the very beginning that it was possible for human beings to grasp the very central core of reality — which he would call its essence. For this very reason he was looked upon by many of his contemporaries as nothing more than a repeater of scholastic thought and was scorned accordingly. It takes but little reflection to realize that the essence of which Husserl speaks throughout his works has very little in common with the essence as we find it in scholastic philosophy. In one sense the Husserlian and the scholastic essences agree; they agree in considering that the central reality, the "what" a thing is, should be looked upon as the very essence of the thing under con-

1. Cf. *Ideen I*, 124, 139, 154, 171.

sideration. This is ultimately that toward which the intellect is primarily oriented in its consideration of that which it knows. Apart from the fact, however, that the scholastic is generally looked upon as a realist while Husserl by his own admission is an idealist, the scholastic belongs to the broad stream which we can call Aristotelianism, and he belongs to it, so to speak, by inclination; whereas Husserl, also by inclination, belongs to that other broad stream which we can call Platonism. There is, in fact, a sense in which Husserl, as Dilthey says, is a thoroughgoing Platonist. For him essence is truly an eternal essence, precisely because it is completely independent of existence in any sense of that much misused word. A thing, an event, an action, or a thought, is what it is whether or not it is. It is possible to know what something is without any reference at all to whether it is or not. There is, thus, no question of "abstracting" essence from empirical reality. Essence, then, is not a capacity for existence; it is simply the reality which, if it exists, is no different from the same reality not existing. With Kant, Husserl sees no intelligible difference at all between one hundred real and one hundred possible thalers. For the scholastic, essence is the source of intelligibility in anything; for Husserl, it is the very intelligibility itself: essence and intelligibility are convertible, and existence as an impediment to intelligibility must be screened out, before any philosophical investigation can properly begin. To say that one has grasped the essence of something is to say that one has grasped its meaning. Thus, for Husserl essence and "sense" are strictly identical. True knowledge of reality, then, is the knowledge of the sense of, the signification of, things. But the sense of things, their signification, is not to be found in a contingent world of things existing independently of consciousness; it is to be found precisely in consciousness itself, where admittedly significance is concentrated. Kant had made it clear, and in this Husserl agrees with Kant, that the sense of things is precisely contributed to them by the consciousness which a subject has of them.

It is not strange, then, that Husserl should look for the essence of reality in consciousness. Nor is it strange that he should be convinced that a grasp of essence in this sense should be knowledge in the very strictest sense; only in consciousness can there be the sort of fixity whereby an object cannot "become" other than it is, thus rendering "knowledge" of it to that extent false. Having defined knowledge as the grasp of that which is necessary, Husserl is quite consistent in thinking that the removal of all that is contingent from the object of consciousness leaves only that which is absolutely necessary. Furthermore, to speak of that which is absolutely necessary is to speak of essence, since, again by definition, essence is that which is what it is, independently of whether or not it is. But, only pure intelligibility has this sort of complete independence. By a sort of tautology which he himself does not seem to have recognized, Husserl has simply defined the necessary as that which has been purified of all contingency — and this "purification" can be accomplished only within consciousness. The whole of Husserl's philosophy, then, can be summed up as an attempt to get at pure intelligibility by simply eliminating all possible obstacles to intelligibility. There is much of which we are already convinced before we begin to philosophize, and for Husserl the task of the philosopher is to investigate the intelligibility of these pre-philosophical convictions. In this, of course, he differs little from most philosophers. Where he differs is in his determination to achieve pure intelligibility by confining himself to an investigation of consciousness, where alone essences can reside.

The Struggle Against Naturalism and Psychologism

The first book which Husserl published after his "conversion" to philosophy was the *Philosophy of Arithmetic*.[2] In this book Husserl the mathematician attempts a sort of philosophy of numbers. To him, a philosophy of numbers is a study of the subjective source whence are derived number-concepts. Since this is a very early work, written at a time when Husserl was still very much under the influence of the psychology of his day, it is largely psychological in its approach. The intention, however, is not to determine the psycho-

2. *Philosophie der Arithmetik* ([only Vol. I was published] Halle, 1891).

logical functions which are at the source of numeration; rather, it is to understand number precisely as that which has been operated by consciousness in its perception of numerable objects. Not that numbers as such can be perceived, but there is a manner of perceiving connected with the operation of "numbering," so that there is an "experience" in which numbers are "given." According to Husserl, it is not from a study of the objects themselves that we will be able to determine what number is, but it is rather from a study of the concepts which consciousness itself has, so to speak, produced that we will understand the very essence of number. All things can be numbered, and, depending on the point of view which the numbering subject adopts, things as various as a thought, an angel, the moon, and an event can be numbered in such a way that from this combination the mind can use the number four in describing its objects. Here there is no interest in the essences of the objects which are numbered; there is an interest only in the essence of the number which the mind imposes upon them.

It had of course been fairly obvious to thinkers for a long time that number is precisely a construct of the mind. But for Husserl this was only a beginning. If it was possible to get at the very essence of number by analyzing the concept of number, why should it not be possible to get at the very essence of anything known simply by examining the concept of that which is known.[3] This, of course, would demand a great deal of preliminary spadework in determining exactly what was to be meant by concept, and what by consciousness were only another thing, then concepts or ideas, which are the products of consciousness, could only be things likewise. able function and no more, then, according to Husserl, consciousness would simply belong to a class of objects which can all be gathered under the heading of things or "facts."[4] If, however, consciousness were only another thing, then concepts or ideas, which are the products of consciousness, could only be things likewise.

---

3. Thus from the very beginning, Husserl has made the same decision as Kant— to limit the intelligibility of "things" to what can be conceptualized.

4. Among the authors whom Husserl read with genuine care was Locke, whom he considers the father of "naturalism" in philosophy.

And if ideas are things, then they are simply contingent facts with no more necessity to them than any other contingent fact, and the possibility of knowledge in any intelligible sense of that term is simply lost. This, according to Husserl, is the road to skepticism, since to wipe out the necessary is to wipe out the very possibility of knowledge.

Like Kant, Husserl is emotionally incapable of accepting skepticism. Nowhere in his writing does he "prove" that there must be knowledge; he simply refuses to recognize even the possibility that there might not be.[5] If, then, he is absolutely sure that there is knowledge, he is equally sure that knowledge is possible only if it **is possible completely to eliminate contingency in any form. Now, to eliminate the contingent is to eliminate from consideration the factual. If consciousness and ideas belong to the realm of the factual, then, in eliminating the factual, one has eliminated consciousness** and ideas too. We might say, then, that from the very beginning Husserl is committed to the only other alternative. Only if consciousness belongs to a world completely separated from the world of fact can consciousness be the seat of knowledge.[6] If it is possible so to purify consciousness that its content can truly be called knowledge, then the object of this kind of consciousness will be a necessary object, which is to say it will be *being* in the only completely true sense of the term. But, to grasp being in the completely true sense of this term is to grasp being as absolutely necessary, and to grasp being as absolutely necessary is to grasp the very *essence* of being. This, then, is for Husserl what philosophy is: a study of being. It is not, however, just any study of being; it is an "essential" study of being, which is but another way of saying, a study whose concern is the essence of things.

Not all this, of course, is to be found in the *Philosophie der Arithmetik*. It is not, in fact, to be found in any of Husserl's early works.

5. Like Plato in the *Theaetetus,* Husserl is well aware that ultimately the conviction that there is knowledge is an act of faith.

6. For Kant this separation of the world of fact from that of consciousness led to the peculiar dualism of *noumenon* and *phenomenon*. Because Husserl refuses this dualism, his philosophy becomes a "pure" phenomenology: the world of fact is not *another* world; it simply *is not.*

Still, looking back from the vantage point of Husserl's mature thought, it is possible to see the seeds of all that is to follow right there at the beginning. This is even more true, if we consider Husserl's monumental *Logical Investigations,*[7] the first edition of which appeared in 1900 and immediately drew the attention of the learned world to their author. It is only with the *Logical Investigations* that the import of "phenomenology" begins to break through; and even here the characterization of phenomenology in the Preface to the second volume as "descriptive psychology" obscured the fundamentally metaphysical intent of the program which was being outlined. This characterization was corrected in 1903[8] (which incidentally seems to be the period when Husserl read Descartes' *Meditations*),[9] and with the correction apparently went a decision to drop the proposed second volume of the *Philosophie der Arithmetik* and to revise the second volume of the *Logical Investigations.* The first volume of the *Logical Investigations* — which in four editions was never appreciably revised — Husserl entitled *Prolegomena to Pure Logic.* It was at one and the same time a violent attack against any purely psychological or functional explanation of the contents of consciousness and a spirited defense of the true ideality and objectivity of the concepts which the mind has.

Husserl is unbending in his rejection of any merely psychological explanation of logical concepts, whether it be that of Locke's empiricism, John Stuart Mill's sensualism, or the functional psychologism of Herbart, Wundt, or the contemporary psychologists of the Vienna school. Rather he would take his cue from Descartes, or Leibniz, or the nineteenth-century German philosopher Bernard

7. Volume I, better known as the *Prolegomena zur reinen Logik,* has been mentioned already. Volume II contains the actual investigations; it was considerably revised in 1913.

8. "Bericht über deutsche Schriften zur Logik aus den Jahren 1895-99," *Archiv für systematische Philosophie,* IX (1903), 397-400. Cf. *Philosophie als strenge Wissenschaft,* p. 318, n. 1.

9. There seems little likelihood that Husserl studied the *Meditations* seriously prior to 1904. In his private library now conserved in the Husserl Archives, Louvain, there is a heavily annotated (only the first two Meditations) German edition, published in 1904. It is only after this that the influence of the *Meditations* shows itself in Husserl's writings.

Bolzano, for whom the realm of ideas was completely separated from the world of fact.[10] As a mathematician Husserl could not but be impressed by the fact that a mathematical formulation was true, eternally true, whether or not it had ever been thought of previously by any human being or whether it might in the future be forgotten by all human beings. This kind of truth must be independent of the factual minds which think it, and hence it must have a being which is independent of factual psychological function on the part of man.[11] There are, of course, no thoughts without a mind to think them, but it is only the existence of the thoughts which depend on the mind; the validity [12] of the thought is something entirely independent of the thinking mind. And, if the concepts which are in consciousness have an independence of the psychological functions of man, then consciousness in the strict sense must also belong to a world which is independent of psychological functioning. A logic is pure precisely to the extent that it is independent of the mind in which it resides. A proposition is true, not because a mind functioned properly in enunciating it, but simply because in itself it has validity.[13] The laws of logic are not laws of thinking, they are laws of thought, which is to say they do not permit us to determine when a mind is thinking properly but rather when the thoughts which a mind has, are true thoughts.

In the *Prolegomena to Pure Logic,* Husserl's battle is with those who claim that the whole of logic can be reduced to a study of mental processes. These men, according to Husserl, have simply "naturalized" ideas and consciousness itself; they have failed to realize that the world of consciousness and the world of fact are

10. In his early days Husserl seems even to have been fascinated by Bolzano's peculiarly "Platonic" notion of a "proposition-in-itself." Cf. *Logische Untersuchungen,* I, No. 35, No. 47, p. 175; Bolzano, *Wissenschaftslehre,* I (Leipzig, 1929), 81–83, 111–13, 143.

11. One is reminded of Plato's discussion of mathematical "realities" in the allegory of the "divided line."

12. Here we have a first hint of the identification of validity (*Gültigkeit*) with being.

13. Even Kant seems at times to have confused the "laws" of logic with those of psychology in his discussion of a priori necessity. This, according to Husserl, is the besetting sin of the neo-Kantians.

completely distinct and separate.[14] Like Plato, like Plotinus, like Augustine, Husserl is fascinated by the eternality of truth; it is true that two plus two equals four, it was true before ever a human mind thought of it, it will be true when no human mind ever thinks of it again. Just what this truth is, just what sort of being can be said of it, is not completely clear and never will be completely clear in the writings of Husserl. But Husserl is completely clear in rejecting the opinions of those who would make this truth, this being, dependent on the minds of those who think it. In all this, one is reminded of Aristotle's interpretation of Plato according to which Plato saw eternal essences existing somehow independently of all particular realizations of them. All of which might well be true, were it not that neither Plato nor Husserl ever conceived these essences in terms of separated existence. These essences, it is true, were conceived as having a being independent of existence, but who could be so foolish as to conceive of them as having an existence independent of existence? It is here that we see the importance of the seemingly simple German word which Husserl uses to characterize the kind of being which essences have. He sees in them not an existence but a *Geltung,* which is to say a validity whereby they can be thought of and spoken of truly. That which is valid can be thought of, and it can be thought of with truth, even though it be impossible to point out any correspondence between the thought and some factual reality. Its being, as an object of thought, is somehow *other* than the operation of thought itself; its very "transcendence" as an object lies in its *exceeding* the thinking which, psychologically speaking, "produced" it.[15]

In 1911, between the first and second editions of the *Logical Investigations,* Husserl published an article entitled "Philosophy as a Strict Science." [16] In this article he took up once more the battle begun in the *Prolegomena to Pure Logic.* Ostensibly the article purported to defend the position that philosophy can and should be a

---

14. Cf. *supra,* p. 24, n. 6.
15. *Die Idee der Phänomenologie,* ed. Walter Biemel (The Hague, Martinus Nijhoff, 1950).
16. See *supra,* Chap. 1, p. 10, n. 8.

strict science. More than that, however, its intention was to show that a strict science of philosophy was possible only if consciousness and ideas were not "naturalized" in the way which the "psychologists" were accustomed to do. It had been the contention of the psychologists that, if philosophy were to be a strict science, it had to be an empirical science since no other discipline merited the name of science at all. And, if philosophy were to be empirical science it could only be a science of the observable psychological functions of man.[17] Now, Husserl would not attack this position by asserting that psychology was not a strict science; he would simply deny that it was a science which could be equated with philosophy. If philosophy was to be a science, which is to say if it was to be philosophy at all, it had to be an *ideal* science, since it was concerned with objects which are not measurable, in the sense in which empirical objects are measurable. Thus the very object of philosophy belongs to a different world from that of the object which other merely empirical sciences considered. The object of philosophy was not factual, it was ideal, and as ideal it sprang from a consciousness which could not be described in empirical terms and which constituted a world all its own. A strict science of philosophy was possible, not because philosophy could be reduced to an empirical science, but because it was possible to attain to a scientific knowledge of the ideal objects which belong in consciousness and in consciousness alone — objects which, in other contexts, Husserl calls "essences."

Husserl's article on the strict science of philosophy is not fully convincing in its efforts to make philosophy purely scientific, but it is convincing as the statement of a position which, in a long life of philosophical thinking and writing, Husserl never really retracted.[18] He did not conceive of this scientific philosophy, or the

17. For the psychologists "introspection" (*Selbstbeobachtung*) cannot be genuine "observation" (*Beobachtung*) and is, hence, inadmissible in "scientific" philosophy. Husserl will reject introspection for an entirely different reason, *i.e.,* that it is just as "naturalistic" as observation.

18. In a manuscript catalogued at Louvain as K III 9 we find the words (p. 79), "Philosophie als strenge Wissenschaft, der Traum ist ausgeträumt." It seems clear, however, that this statement does not apply to the ideal so much as to the possibility of soliciting the support necessary from likeminded scholars to implement the ideal.

philosophical science, as something easy of accomplishment. But he definitely did consider it as something which could be accomplished, and this precisely because he was convinced that it was possible to strip consciousness of all those factual and hence contingent elements which militated against the truly scientific character of the knowledge it should possess. In 1911, however, this complete purification of consciousness was still in the distant ideal future. Husserl's whole life as well as his whole philosophy can be looked upon as a constant vision of the possibility of accomplishing purification.

The first steps toward the accomplishment of this purification are, we might say, accomplished in the second edition of the second volume of the *Logical Investigations,* wherein he undertakes the painful task of analyzing the very significations which the mind grasps in its view of the objects presented to it. Logical classifications are quite obviously not "discovered" as though contained in the objects of thought prior to any logical analysis; nor are they mere arbitrarily "constructed" entities. They are somewhere between these two extremes, and a clarification of their genesis will provide for Husserl the key to a complete analysis of the objective side of consciousness. In the attempt to explicate logical classifications, particularly in Investigations I and V of this second volume, Husserl develops a concept which is to prove the most important concept in his whole subsequent philosophy.

It is the concept of intentionality, which he had taken from his former teacher Franz Brentano, who had in turn taken it from his intensive studies in scholastic philosophy. In the above-mentioned Investigations, Husserl undertakes an analysis of meanings. It is significant that the German word *Meinung,* which signifies either opinion or meaning, has the same stem as the German verb *meinen* which signifies to intend. Thus, in his analysis of meaning, Husserl comes to the conclusion that to mean signifies to intend and that, therefore, a meaning is an intention of the mind. In general we might say that an intention is some sort of immanent term of the mind's operation when the mind is related in one way or another to some object. For Brentano, on the one hand, intentionality signified little more than the relationship which the mind has to some extramental reality. For Husserl, on the other hand, intentionality refers not only to the mind's relationship but also to the term of that relationship, which is as intramental as is the operation itself.[19] It is somewhat paradoxical that Husserl, whose whole orientation is rather antischolastic, should in this manner have a concept of intention and of intentionality which is far closer to that of the scholastics than is that of Brentano, whose early training was entirely in the scholastic tradition. At any rate, the whole of the *Logical Investigations* can be looked upon as an attempt on the part of Husserl to analyze precisely this objective contribution of the mind to that which the mind itself knows.[20] Ultimately, the very essence of being itself will be found in this objective term of the mind's operation; but at this early stage Husserl is concerned only with making it clear that there is such an objective term, or intention, and that logic, whose function is to lay down the rules of thought, is to be a study of traditional logical concepts precisely from the point of view of the mind's operational function in which they originate.[21] However, since thought is expressed in language, an analysis of language can provide the key for an analysis of thought. Now, such a language analysis reveals that expression is made up of two elements, which we may call its physical configuration (either written or oral) and its meaning. And, continues Husserl, this meaning is so completely distinct from the physical configuration that it simply belongs to an entirely different world. The world of physical configuration is the world of *fact,* whereas the world of meaning is the world of consciousness, which is but another way of saying the world of *intentions.* One can, by a physical operation,

19. Only later does Husserl express this theoretically in treating of the relations between noesis and noema (*Ideen I*, Nos. 87–96).

20. From the very beginning, Husserl tries to get away from the merely formal a priori contribution to the cognitive synthesis recognized by Kant.

21. To the extent that Husserl's logic investigates objective concepts within a framework of subjective operations it is, of course, psychological, but to the extent that his logic is not based on an observation of psychological "behaviors," Husserl will call it a "pure" or "immanent" psychology — which refuses to look on consciousness as a "thing." See "Phenomenology," *Encyclopaedia Britannica*, Vol. XVII (14th ed., 1929), cols. 699–702; *Philosophie als strenge Wissenschaft.*

write or speak a word; but only by an operation of consciousness can one give to it a meaning. Now, there is nothing terribly new in all this; but there is something very new in the connection which Husserl makes between meaning, sense, and essence. And there is something even newer in the fact that all of these are joined together through the common bond of intentionality.

Although Husserl begins his logical analyses with an analysis of language, which is after all the externalization of thought, his primary purpose is to analyze precisely that element of language which is primarily the product of the mind. This element, as we said, is the meaning which the mind gives to its expressions. A meaning, however, by the mere fact that it is a meaning is not necessarily true. In fact, it has been perfectly obvious to thinkers for centuries that it is quite possible for the mind to signify something without there being any justifiable correspondence between that meaning and the way things actually are. To say this is nothing more than to recognize that there is such a thing as error. If, then, a meaning is to be a true meaning, it must be more than merely an intention of the mind; it must be an intention which is verified, validated, or justified.[22]

At this early stage in his thoughts, Husserl speaks of an intention which has not been justified as a *mere* intention or an intention of signification. A mere intention is an "empty" intention. When it has been verified, validated, or justified, it is then a "filled" intention. Most of Husserl's analyses of meaning are devoted precisely to determining what this "filling" or fulfillment of empty intentions is. Without going into the details of the long and somewhat tortuous analyses of the six *Logical Investigations,* we can say that an intention is filled if it rests not merely on the meaning which the mind *gives* in thinking but upon an "intuition," which is but another way of saying that it rests upon an experience of that which the mind signifies in thought. For example, one can hear another speak of a white house with green shutters on the southwest corner of Main Street and Fourth Avenue. All of that description can carry

22. Here, once more, we see that Husserl has made his decision against the Platonic–Aristotelian notion of truth.

a meaning to the one who hears it, but, according to Husserl, this is but an empty meaning, if the hearer does not have an intuition — whether through perception or through imagination — of all the elements of the description.[23] Each of the elements, we might say, is an intention wherein some characteristic of the actual state of affairs is signified. If, however, an intuition, wherein the said characteristic is actually "seen," does not correspond to each element of the discription, then the intention, wherein the whole is signified, is to that extent not filled but empty. It is not necessary that one *perceive* or even *have perceived* that which is intended; it is sufficient that one have a clear picture of it in imagination. One can look at a cube, for example, and have a perfectly valid intention of cubes, but such an intention would not be valid, if the subject in question had no intuition of any kind regarding those sides of the cube which cannot be seen in a single perception. On the other hand, since a filled intention is not one in which the *existence* of the object in question is given it is not necessary that the other sides of the cube be actually perceived by the subject; it is enough that he have an intuition of cube as that which has the other sides. In such an intuition, one sees the *essence* of cube — whether or not there be a cube at all.[24]

An analysis of meaning on this level is, of course, extremely superficial, but it leads to what Husserl considers the very heart of all logical analysis, namely the return to that which is the ultimate source of any meaning whatever. Take the most elaborate theory conceivable: it is, according to Husserl, nothing but a mumbo-jumbo of arbitrary constructions unless the theorist returns to the ultimate intuitions wherein all the elements of his theory are *given* and not merely signified by his own mind. An object is *given* if it is genuinely the object of an intuition; otherwise it is merely signified by the mind and has no real justification whatever. If, on the other hand, it is genuinely given, then it is given as what it is, which

23. Husserl is by no means saying, against both Aristotle and Kant, that there can be truth where there is no judgment. As we shall see later, he will ultimately broaden the notion of judgment to take in the non-predicative.

24. Neither here nor later does Husserl have much to say about the "matter of fact" or "existential" judgment, presumably because, with Hume, he sees no question of "knowledge" in such judgments.

is to say, its essence is given. Obviously, an essence given in this way can be more or less perfectly given, but if it is the essence which is given, then the mind actually *sees* the essence and does not merely signify it vaguely. Since the whole of philosophy is to consist for Husserl in seeing essences as they are, this can be looked upon as the beginning of a long program of searching for essences: in his own words, a program of "bringing essences to givenness."[25] If he can develop a method whereby it will be possible to *see* essences, not only the simple essences of cube, the color red, the note C, etc., but also the essences of all the complexities which the mind is capable of understanding — of logical concepts, of scientific theories, of aesthetic, moral, or religious values, of social or political structures — in short, of all those things of which men speak without knowing thoroughly of what they speak, then Husserl's goal will have been attained. This is the goal of a philosophy which is truly scientific because it has done away with all mere opinions and has transformed them into knowledge.[26] In order to achieve this goal, Husserl felt that it was necessary to begin by a purification of psychology, to rid it of its exclusive concern with the factual, to make of it a discipline in which the very essence of consciousness and of its intentions could be determined.

Phenomenology as an A Priori Psychological Discipline

In the Preface to this second edition I have discussed the change in the situation regarding translations of Husserl's works since 1958. There can be no question that the English-speaking public is now in a far better position to gain first-hand acquaintance with Husserl's thought than it then was. All the problems are not solved, however, both because of the unevenness of the translations and because of the difficulty of following Husserl's thought in even the best of translations. Perhaps the best introduction to Husserl's style of thinking — particularly its "anti-naturalistic" bent and its insistence on the purely ideal being of both human consciousness and its intentional objects

---

25. *Philosophie als strenge Wissenschaft*, p. 301.

26. To this extent, at least, Husserl's aim, as he claims in *Philosophie als strenge Wissenschaft* (p. 292), is the same as Plato's. It is doubtful, however, that Plato (particularly the Plato of the later dialogues) would accept this distinction between knowledge and opinion.

— can be found in an article entitled "Philosophie als strenge Wissenschaft," [27] which Husserl published in 1911, in the international philosophical journal *Logos*. At this point, however, I should like to call attention to the article "Phenomenology" which Husserl contributed for the fourteenth edition of the *Encyclopaedia Britannica*. Even though the article is severely truncated, giving only approximately one-third of what Husserl originally wrote, it nevertheless provides a fairly good introduction into the kind of thought which can be called phenomenological, in the sense in which Husserl himself understood the term. For anyone who has no acquaintance at all with Husserl's thought it is not an easy article to read. It does, however, provide an outline into which can be fitted some of the important themes of the phenomenological approach to philosophy. It is here that Husserl defines phenomenology as an "a priori psychological discipline," [28] which provides the only secure basis for a scientific psychology. This is but another way of saying that psychology itself can be scientific only if all the concepts it employs have been investigated according to the phenomenological method, wherein the very essences which these concepts represent are revealed to the investigator.[29] Thus, when Husserl in the same article defines phenomenology as a universal philosophy which is the basis for all sciences, he is not rejecting the first definition given; he is simply indicating his conviction that the phenomenological method is the only basis on which one can construct a genuine science of any kind, since only by phenomenology can one grasp the essences with which one is concerned in any particular science. Since, too, Husserl had more than once indicated his dissatisfaction with any sort of philosophical "system," it is evident that for him philosophy

27. Edmund Husserl, *Phenomenology and the Crisis of Philosophy*, trans. with an Introduction by Quentin Lauer (New York: Harper & Row, 1965). The second essay, "Philosophy and the Crisis of European Man," since it was delivered almost *ex tempore* as a lecture and was only cursorily edited for publication, will be read with rather more difficulty.

28. Cf. *Philosophie als strenge Wissenschaft*, p. 296. It is this sort of thing which led many of Husserl's contemporaries to stigmatize him as "scholastic," thus showing that they understood neither Husserl nor the scholastics.

29. This does not contradict Husserl's rejection of the qualification "descriptive psychology" (cf. *supra*, p. 25, n. 8). In the sense in which he had formerly understood psychology, phenomenology is not psychology at all.

will have to begin somewhere and verify or validate all the concepts which are used,[30] particularly in those sciences which are most closely allied with what is generally looked upon as philosophy. Thus, if being in consciousness is to be at the very core of all philosophy, and if the intentions whereby objects are signified are to be the functions of consciousness, then the first step in philosophy will be the study of consciousness, and the first step in this study will be the determination of precisely what consciousness is, which is to say, what is the *essence* of consciousness.

More definitively than in his early works Husserl in this article admits that, since psychology is a science of the psychical, and since the psychical is in some sense a part of animal nature, psychology is in some sense, then, a science of nature or a natural science. The question, however, is whether psychology can proceed in such a way as to purify the psychical of all the natural elements which accompany it in its operation, to such an extent that it will be possible to speak of a purely psychical science. Such a science would be concerned exclusively with acts of consciousness and not at all with the physical concomitants which inevitably accompany it in its operation. If such a science be possible, the objects with which it is concerned can certainly not be grasped according to the method of any known natural sciences, since they are wedded to the factual, upon which all their experiments are based.[31]

Although Husserl has a rather extraordinary prejudice against Hegel, the insight with which his own phenomenology begins is very similar to that of Hegel himself. According to Hegel, so long as consciousness is simply consciousness of something outside itself it cannot be properly scientific; to be scientific it must ultimately be consciousness of consciousness itself. Now, though Husserl would most vehemently reject the dialectical process whereby, ac-

---

30. Like Hegel, Husserl is very much concerned with freeing the "beginning" of philosophy from all arbitrariness; only thus can it be scientific. As we shall see later, it is only by redefining "rational" that he can accomplish this.

31. Husserl would not eliminate all investigation of behaviors from a properly psychological discipline. He will, however, not recognize such investigations as scientific, until they become phenomenological — thereby completing the divorce between experience and existence. But that is a later chapter.

cording to Hegel, one goes from consciousness to consciousness of consciousness, his conviction that only acts of consciousness can be objects of scientific knowledge in the strict sense is strangely reminiscent of Hegel.[32] To be conscious of consciousness itself, however, is to reflect; and thus, for Husserl, the primary philosophical act is the act of reflection. Since, apparently, unlike Hegel, Husserl never felt the need of breaking out of the reflexive circle, he never felt the need of a method which would not only be reflexive but also dialectical. Though Husserl himself never mentions it, his concept of reflection reminds one to a great extent of Fichte's starting point.[33] To understand being is to understand the consciousness in which being in its fullness resides; and to understand the consciousness in which being in its fullness resides is ultimately to understand the self as subject, without which objects would not be objects. Thus, we can see, there is even in Husserl's thought a dialectic; but it is the more static dialectic of Fichte rather than the dynamic dialectic of Hegel.[34] In any event it is clear that for Husserl, since a psychical experience (or act) can be grasped only in reflection, then to philosophize is not to examine the things of which one is conscious, but rather to examine the very consciousness one has of them; consciousness, of course, being understood as "pure" not "psychological" consciousness.

To speak of consciousness, however, is not to speak of the activity whereby a subject is conscious; rather it is to speak of a mode of being, the mode of being which things have when we are conscious of them. If, now, we return to the terminology of Kant, we find that the being which something can be thought to have independently of consciousness is called its being-in-itself, whereas the being which it has in consciousness is called its appearance or phenomenal being. Thus, to say that philosophy must examine the consciousness

32. One is tempted to suspect that Husserl fails to be adequately "scientific" precisely because he eliminates the "mediation," which Hegel found necessary.

33. It is known that Husserl occupied himself seriously with Fichte for several years at Göttingen.

34. The limitations of this sort of dialectic will be seen later, when Husserl wrestles with the insoluble problem of intersubjectivity in a purely transcendental framework.

of things[35] is but another way of saying that it should examine the appearance of things, *i.e.,* the being they have when they appear.

It is characteristic of phenomenology that it cannot even say what it is itself, or what a phenomenon is, without first applying the phenomenological method in order thereby to know its own essence — only through the phenomenological method can we know the essence of anything, even of phenomenology itself. Thus, the phenomenological method necessarily antedates the science of phenomenology, since the latter could not be truly scientific unless it is first of all phenomenological.[36]

As early as the *Logical Investigations,* Husserl sought to discover the essence of consciousness — understanding it as an *act* of being conscious, rather than as a *faculty* for being conscious.[37] And he came to the conclusion that all consciousness is necessarily "consciousness-of" something. In speaking thus, he was saying that the "of" is inseparable from every act of consciousness, which was but another way of saying that consciousness is essentially oriented toward an object.[38] Now, this orientation, which is to be found in every act of consciousness, is its *intentionality,* which is discovered, not by some impossible analysis of what is outside consciousness, but simply from an analysis of consciousness itself. Thus, without emerging from the reflexive circle, Husserl is convinced that he can discover all that is to be discovered regarding both subjectivity and

35. It is misleading to translate the German *Bewusstsein* by "consciousness," since the English in no way indicates a special mode of being. The flexibility of the German is further highlighted by Heidegger's development, in *Sein und Zeit,* of *Vorhandensein, Zuhandensein,* and *Dasein:* like *Bewusstsein* each indicates, by including the element of *sein,* that it describes a mode of being.

36. It is, of course, true of any philosophy — and not merely of Marxism — that in it practice must precede theory, since theory is, so to speak, the crystallization of practice.

37. Like the English "consciousness," the German *Bewusstsein* can mean both. Nor can language alone dictate which aspect is to be emphasized — a fact which phenomenologists sometimes tend to forget.

38. For Sartre this means that the essence of consciousness is to be the opposite of being, i.e., non-being, *néant:* "Dire que la conscience est conscience de quelque chose cela signifie qu'il n'y a pas d'être pour la conscience en dehors de cette obligation précise d'être intuition révélante de quelque chose, c'est-à-dire d'un être transcendant." *L'être et le néant* (Paris: Gallimard, 1948), pp. 28–29.

objectivity — neither of which has significance without the other.

It is important to recognize that the kind of reflection which Husserl sees as the primary philosophical act is utterly distinct from the sort of *introspection* whereby one looks within oneself and examines or seeks to analyze what has taken place in the line of conscious activity.[39] To examine consciousness introspectively is, according to the phenomenologists, to falsify consciousness, since it means immobilizing that which is essentially vital.[40] A living act cannot be objectified in the way *things* can be objectified; an act of consciousness can be grasped correctly only by being "lived." This, incidentally, is the reason why knowledge of the psychical must be entirely different from knowledge of the physical. Thus, whatever belongs to the psychical realm can be grasped only by a special kind of experience which Husserl calls an *Erlebnis* or "vital experience." This means that true reflection is inseparable from that which is reflected upon, since the former is but a more profound "living" of the latter. If, for example, I look out my window and see a tree, it can be said that I am conscious of a tree. I cannot, however, be said to know *what* a tree is until I live reflexively my own consciousness of tree. There may or may not be a tree out there, which exists independently of its appearing to me; still, there is only one source whence I can derive an *essential* knowledge of tree, and that is the act of consciousness wherein the tree appears to me. I become aware of what a tree is essentially, not in examining the psychological function whereby I am or become aware of the tree, but in living my awareness more deeply. Later phenomenologists, such as Dietrich von Hildebrand, for example, have pointed out that phenomenology does not necessarily seek new knowledge but only a new and more profound realization of the knowledge which one already has.[41] This new realization or living profoundly one's awareness they have characterized as a "prise de conscience."

39. Cf. *supra*, p. 28, n. 17.

40. Cf. Brentano, *Psychologie vom empirischen Standpunkt*, I (Vienna, 1873), 45–46; Husserl, *Philosophie als strenge Wissenschaft*, p. 306; Scheler, *Der Formalismus in der Ethik und die materiale Wertethik*, pp. 397–401.

41. To this extent, at least, the phenomenologists have inserted themselves firmly in the Platonic tradition.

To be aware of one's own conscious act is to have an *Erlebnis* in its regard; and to be aware of one's own consciousness as objectively oriented (in this case as containing the object "tree") is to have an "intentional *Erlebnis*," which, according to Husserl, is the act of consciousness in the strict sense of the term "act." Thus, adequately to describe an *act* (as opposed to an *activity*) of consciousness, it is not sufficient to say either that it is oriented toward an object or that it is *lived* in reflection; it must be a reflexive living of one's own consciousness precisely as intentional or objectively oriented. When one approaches appearances or "phenomena" in this way, one finds in them all that is necessary for the constitution of a *strict science* of that which is.[42]

It is in this sense that phenomenology is to be understood. An act of consciousness is that in which an object "appears"; it is the "appearance" of an object. If one prescinds from the whole question of whether this object also "exists" independently of consciousness — and this, according to Husserl, we must do, since such existing would be at best contingent and thus of no import to *strict* science[43] — then, with nothing but the act of consciousness to go on, one can determine adequately the essence of that which is in consciousness. Since, too, the being of an object in consciousness is its appearance or "phenomenon," essential knowledge needs no more than phenomena in order to be adequate. Quite obviously essential knowledge would be utterly insignificant if it remained at this elementary level, but if, as Husserl says, "each phenomenon has its own structure, which analysis shows to be an ever-widening system of individually intentional and intentionally related components," [44] then there is no essence, however complex, which cannot be understood by an analysis of the intentions present in the act wherein the object is

42. According to Heidegger, it is only of "that which is" (*das Seiende*) that there can be *science*. For a grasp of "being" (*das Sein*) something better is required — and this something better is for Heidegger philosophy. Cf. *Brief über den Humanismus* (Frankfurt am Main: Klostermann, 1949).

43. A denial of independent existence, which Husserl finds in Berkeley's metaphysics, would be just as illegitimate, since "strict science" permits no position at all with regard to existence.

44. "Phenomenology," *Encyclopaedia Britannica*, XVII, col. 700.

present to consciousness. To know one's intentions completely is to know reality completely in the only way in which it can be known.[45]

In one sense all this is not so very different from the scholastic approach to knowledge. For the scholastic, being as *known* is simply an exact counterpart of being as it is in reality. Since, then, it is clear that an *analysis* of being as it is in reality is meaningless, an analysis of being as known is considered to be an exact knowledge of what reality is. Husserl simply leaves out the counterpart — he has no patience with dualism — and thus refuses to consider any such thing as being as it is in reality. This he does for two reasons: first, because he agrees with Kant who says there is no way of determining whether or not there is exact correspondence; and, secondly, because he simply is not concerned with correspondence in the existential order. All the knowledge he wants, which is a strict knowledge of essence, is revealed in consciousness — a knowledge which is valid, whether or not essences *exist*. Since it is possible for such things as tree not to exist, Husserl is convinced that their existence or nonexistence is not important, for he knows exactly what he "means" by tree, and in this he has a truly scientific knowledge of the essence of tree.

It is not, however, true that Husserl reduces all philosophy to an analysis of meanings — he had no desire to be a logical positivist. His whole theory of experience and of intuition is such that he can at one and the same time recognize the subjective source of all intentions and still deny in them any arbitrariness. When properly analyzed, intentions are revealed as truly objective, which is to say that to have an essential knowledge of what one *means* by tree is to know what all others must mean by tree if they are to be objective.[46] Obviously, Husserl admits that there is such a thing as error

45. Husserl goes back beyond Kant to the Cartesian ideal of complete rationality — no *being* can be allowed to be rationally unknowable. As we shall see later, this involves revamping not only the notion of reason but also that of *being*.

46. It is not easy for phenomenologists to avoid a particular brand of dogmatism in following out this position consistently. One of the few to do so is Gabriel Marcel, who admits that he merely "assumes" that other men's experiences are the same as his own. Cf. *Homo Viator* (Paris: Aubier, 1944), p. 39.

— though it is never quite clear what he can mean by error — but when he speaks of true knowledge he means a knowledge which is truly knowledge precisely because it is not simply constructed by the knowing subject (Husserl has a horror of *pure* subjectivism). It is, in fact, precisely this last element which causes many to doubt the ultimate adequacy of phenomenology, since various phenomenologists defend intuitions which are diverse and sometimes even contradictory. If, however, we are to judge whether phenomenology is or can be satisfactory as a philosophy, we cannot be content with pointing out difficulties of detail; we must follow Husserl through a lifetime of painful analysis. Husserl's theories have been discarded by the realists as too positivistic; by the positivists as too realistic — a fairly good sign that they are neither.[47]

If Husserl is to be consistent, then, he must deliberately confine himself in his analysis to that which is immanent in consciousness. At the same time he must be able to find within the immanence of consciousness a complete justification of the objectivity, or what he calls the "objective validity," of knowledge. Husserl cannot be convinced that he sees things correctly without being convinced that anyone who sees them otherwise is looking at them incorrectly. Ultimately, phenomenology will be a theory of knowledge, according to which knowledge is not true because it corresponds with objective reality, but which sees reality as objective because knowledge of it is true. A true judgment, of course, will continue to be one which expresses the state of things as they are; but it will be necessary to find the criterion for the judgment's truth in the judgment itself and not in the state of things as they are.[48] It must be possible to find within consciousness a criterion for determining whether

---

47. Husserl refers to his own philosophy both as "true positivism" (*Philosophie als strenge Wissenschaft*, p. 340) and as "true realism" (*Nachwort zu meinen Ideen*, p. 14).

48. This is, of course, an early way of stating the problem. In the light of Husserl's developed doctrine it will be possible to state that the only *true* being things have is that which they have in true judgments. This is the lesson of *Formale und transzendentale Logik* (Halle: Niemeyer, 1929) and of *Erfahrung und Urteil* (Prague: Akademia Verlag, 1939). The latter was re-edited in 1948 (Hamburg, Claasen and Goverts).

consciousness intends being correctly. If I want to determine what something really is, I must turn to the experience in which the something is present to my consciousness; therein I will find an intentional structure, and that intentional structure properly analyzed will reveal to me all that can be revealed with regard to the object toward which my experience is oriented. This structure of intentionality is the fundamental structure of any phenomenon; it is present to my consciousness prior to any reflection upon it, but in order to know what the experience of it is and thus to know what is experienced, I must penetrate into all the intentions which make up its structure, and I must do so in such a way as completely to validate these intentions as intentions of this object and of no other.[49] To the extent that one has grasped any object as distinguishable from any other, one has an "essential" grasp of that object.

Since it is quite clearly possible, however, to intend an object in more ways than one, one cannot be said to have analyzed the intentionality operative in the consciousness of an object without having examined the various modes of intending the same object.[50] These modes of intending can be looked upon as modifications of the fundamental structure of intentionality — and only if they are understood in this way will the object be present without distortion. To perceive something, for example, is not the same as to imagine it, or to recall it, or to anticipate it. Although, as we said before, it is possible to grasp the very essence of something through an imaginary image as well as through perception, still, if one is to grasp its essence accurately one must know whether the intention wherein it is present to consciousness is an intention of perception, of imagination, of recall, etc. Here again, however, it is the structure of the conscious act, and not something outside consciousness itself, which reveals to the phenomenological investigator what kind of act is in question. If I raise my eyes from the paper on which I am writing I

49. Philosophical reflection adds nothing to the intentional structure already present in pre-reflexive consciousness. It merely brings to the surface, so to speak, what was already present prior to reflection.

50. *Vorlesungen zur Phänomenologie des inneren Zeitbewusstseins* (Halle: Niemeyer, 1938) is greatly concerned with this problem. Cf. *Logische Untersuchungen*, Vol. II, Part I, pp. 109–10; Vol. II, Part II, p. 220.

can *see* the books in my bookcase. If I then close my eyes I can *imagine* those same books. Finally, if I leave the room I can *recall* having looked at the books and describe more or less accurately the books on my shelves. No one would hesitate to say that I have *intended* the same books in three different ways; yet it should be fairly obvious that these three acts are not distinguished by their contents, simply as contents.[51] It is the structure of these acts as acts which differentiates them; and they can be checked one against the other in order to guarantee their accuracy. Nor is this "checking" necessarily all one-sided: not only can imagination and recall be checked against perception; perception itself may need revision, if we find it conflicting with recall or imagination — particularly where an *essential* grasp is in question.

It should be clear, too, that in any complex experience there can be present intentions of different types at one and the same time. These we might call the components of an experiential synthesis, each component having a structure of its own, and each conforming to a type. A complete phenomenological investigation will, then, demand a systematic investigation of types, since no essence can be completely or even adequately revealed unless the intentional structure of the act, wherein the subject is conscious of this essence, is revealed exactly for what it is. Let us suppose that I am standing before a house and looking at it. Do I have a perception of that house or only of its façade? Quite obviously I do not perceive the whole house; and just as obviously I know what a house is. If I do not move, then I have a perception of the house's façade, and with regard to the other sides, I either recall having seen them before, or I imagine what the other sides of a house look like, or I anticipate what they will look like when I do move around to the other side. When, therefore, I look at the house I *intend* it in various ways. So long as I recognize that these are various ways of intending the house, I can synthesize these intentions into one complex intention of house, all the while remaining aware of the character manifested by the component intentions. I can also circle the house and verify

51. The fact that I grasp them with more clarity and detail in one act than in another is not due to a difference in contents *as* contents.

the nonperceptive intentions I had of it. Where, however, the object in question is not quite so simple, it is not always possible to verify nonperceptive intentions by transforming them into perceptive intentions. This still does not mean, according to Husserl, that I cannot have an essential knowledge of an object of this kind. In my search for essential knowledge I am never confined to one or even a few experiences; I can draw on a whole lifetime of experiences, and thus any experience fits into a perpetual flow of consciousness and is colored by the fact that it is not isolated but belongs not only to a spatial but also to a temporal synthesis.[52] In *Phänomenologie des inneren Zeitbewusstseins* (written in 1911, but not published until 1928, when it was edited by Martin Heidegger), Husserl treats at length the "temporality" of every intentional act, containing as it does elements of recall and anticipation in addition to that of perception or imagination. Our experiences in the present are what they are, only because they are colored by our memory of past and anticipation of future experiences. And by this fact, too, the present itself is always temporally extended.

In all this — whether the object in question be some physically perceptible thing, or an event, or a social structure, or even a moral value — the important thing for the phenomenologist is to arrive at an intuition of precisely what the object in question is essentially. Now, this essential intuition cannot be achieved by simply willing to do so; if it could there would be no need of a special method called phenomenology. It has been remarked more than once that the voluminous writings of Husserl, both published and unpublished, contain actually a paucity of distinct phenomenological analyses and therefore of identifiable essential intuitions. This is true, and the reason is that Husserl conceived it as his task to establish the method whereby phenomenological analyses and essential intuitions would be made possible, thus devoting his whole life to the development of a phenomenological program rather than to the actual carrying out of phenomenological analyses, which he hoped would be accomplished, generation after gen-

52. Only in his later writings does Husserl occupy himself to any great extent with the temporal synthesis of experiences.

eration, by a whole community of scholars devoting itself to the sort of method he tried to perfect during his lifetime.[53] Hence, we find him devoting far more time and energy to the elucidation of the techniques which phenomenology is to employ than to the actual employment of those same techniques.[54] If we are to understand not only the theories of Husserl but also the impact which those theories had upon philosophers of his own day and on so much of contemporary philosophy, we must examine in somewhat more detail the principal techniques which he evolved. In doing so we should come to a better knowledge not only of the phenomenological method but also of the very philosophy of being which, in the mind of Husserl, can be called a phenomenology of being.

53. Cf. *Philosophie als strenge Wissenschaft*, pp. 338–39.

54. Even in *Phänomenologie des inneren Zeitbewusstseins*, which is intended as a particular application of a detailed phenomenological analysis, Husserl does not get to the point of analyzing, as he promised, the "objective" concept of time.

BASIC PHENOMENOLOGICAL TECHNIQUES

THE PHENOMENOLOGICAL METHOD as conceived by Husserl is aptly characterized in the title of his last major work published during his lifetime.[1] The occasion for writing this work came with a series of lectures on phenomenology delivered at the Sorbonne in Paris in the year 1929: as a tribute to France's greatest philosopher, Husserl entitled the subsequent publication of these lectures *Cartesian Meditations*. The title is apt, because on the one hand Husserl considered his philosophical ideal as "Cartesian" in a very particular sense, and because on the other hand his method is, in the last analysis, a method of "meditation." In Husserl's opinion the essence of Cartesianism consists in its passion for the rational justification of all knowledge; and his own decision to seek in reason itself this justification is precisely what he constantly refers to as a "pure Cartesianism." Still, since the authenticity of Husserl's Cartesianism is subject to doubt, for us the second part of the title, in which the work is described as a series of "Meditations," takes on a particular importance. It is as though Husserl were saying, "what Descartes attempted [without success] through a technique of deduction based on a single indubitable principle we shall accomplish through a technique of meditation on the same principle correctly understood." It was in the Cartesian *cogito* that Husserl had found those certitudes upon which he was to

1. *Méditations cartésiennes* (Paris: Colin, 1931); re-edited in 1947 (Paris: Vrin). This work appeared originally in the French translation by M. Emmanuel Lévinas and Mlle Gabrielle Peiffer. Not until 1950 did the Husserl Archives in Louvain, under the direction of Father H. Van Breda, bring out the German text, *Cartesianische Meditationen,* ed. S. Strasser (The Hague: Martinus Nijhoff, 1950). It is more complete than the French version and contributes much to a better understanding of transcendental phenomenology. The English translation by Dorion Cairns, *Cartesian Meditations* (The Hague: Nijhoff, 1960), is based on Strasser's edition.

build an entire philosophy, though the key to this whole development was to be the essential intentionality of consciousness, an insight which he had already developed to some extent prior to having read Descartes.[2] What the *cogito* first contributed was an apodictic certitude of the subject, afforded by the very fact of consciousness — not, it is true, the certitude, which Descartes thought he had found, of a substantial subject of consciousness, but rather the certitude of a subjectivity from which all the contingent elements of factuality could be eliminated, leaving only "pure consciousness" or subjectivity as such.[3] The second certitude revealed to him in his reading of Descartes [4] was simply an application of the principle of intentionality to the *cogito*. *Ego cogito* is in itself an empty statement; it is meaningful only when it becomes *ego cogito cogitatum,* but in this form it is fortified with the same certitude as is the fact of consciousness, which is to say, one can be just as certain of the object of consciousness as one is of the fact of consciousness itself.[5] The Cartesian certitude, then, in Husserl's opinion, becomes fruitful only when it is given a content, and it is fruitful precisely because this content is known with the same apodictic certitude as is the *cogito* itself. He insists, in fact, that in this he has been truer to the original intuition of the *cogito* than was Descartes himself.[6]

In order, however, that the certitude of the *cogito* become an objective certitude and in order that meaning be given to the war

2. Husserl seems to have read the first two Meditations, found what he wanted, and stopped there. He completely misses the significance of the *malin génie* and the *veracitas Dei.*

3. Though it is sometimes difficult to see how Husserl avoids the abstractness of Kant's "subjectivity in general," there is no question that he *intended* a concrete subjectivity — a sort of concrete subject standing for all subjectivity (as Berkeleyan as such an interpretation may seem).

4. "Revealed to him in his reading of Descartes" is said advisedly. Husserl admitted more than once (cf. Mss K III 9, pp. 1, 5, 7–8, 87–88; K III 4, pp. 106–107; K III 6, pp. 273–74) that he did not read other philosophers in order to know exactly what they had said, but in order to "find" in them ideas which would serve toward the development of his own philosophy.

5. The condition for this, of course, is minute attention to the intentional structure of the act of consciousness.

6. Cf. *Cartesianische Meditationen,* Nos. 13, 14.

cry of phenomenology in its struggle with positivism, "to things themselves," it was necessary to develop precisely those techniques which would enable the subject to eliminate, both from consciousness and from its object, those elements of contingency which make doubt possible. Though the "meditation" which is philosophy may begin with the "fact" of the *cogito,* it is not until the uncertainty connected with the "factual" had been eliminated, that the original certitude could begin to bear fruit. Thus there were developed in the theory of Husserl those techniques which make his phenomenology a thing apart, which distinguish it ultimately from the phenomenology of his most ardent disciples — for, in the last analysis, Husserl was singularly alone in the full technique which he developed over the years, and it was precisely in the full application of the various techniques he had evolved that he distinguished himself from all others. Not even the introduction in later years into this framework of a certain notion of history — or historicity — could bridge the gap between himself and other phenomenologists.[7]

When Husserl, as we mentioned before, described phenomenology as a "science of essences," he meant by that to indicate two things: first, that it is a science whose objects in no way depend on mental construction; and secondly, that it is one in which the essences known are in no way dependent on the concrete, factual realizations of these essences.[8] In order, then, that there be an "essential" knowledge of things, it becomes necessary both that consciousness be viewed minus the contingent functions which accompany it and that the essences of things be disengaged from all that which is simply accidental to them. The first step in this direction, as we have seen, was Husserl's insistence that essences could be *seen* in appearances or in their very phenomenality. In order, however, that essences be seen in this way, it was necessary to remove from objects all that was not purely phenomenal. What is more, if phenomenology was to be a universal methodology, ap-

7. Quite obviously Husserl is distinguished from all those who think that the mere method of a more or less detailed description of experiences constitutes a phenomenology.

8. In this general form it is a good description of Platonic "essences" or "forms."

plicable to all objects of knowledge, it was necessary to evolve certain techniques aimed at assuring the pure phenomenality of any object of investigation whatsoever, thus making it possible to "see" the essence not only of some things but of all things.

The first and most fundamental of these techniques is negative; it is aimed at eliminating from any object of investigation precisely that factuality which is the root of contingency and hence of doubt.[9] With his peculiar penchant for Greek terminology, Husserl calls this first technique the epoche, which is conceived as a radical and universal elimination of any position of factual existence. It is to be noticed that the epoche was never intended by Husserl to be an elimination of existence itself, since to eliminate existence would be to take a position in its regard, thus exposing oneself to the danger of contingency. Existence, or, as Husserl frequently called it, "transcendence," is simply bracketed ("put in parentheses") in the sense that in its regard no position is taken either for or against — it may be that things exist outside consciousness, but since this existence can have no significance whatever with regard to the essence of things, it is simply left out of consideration.[10] This epoche is clearly in a certain sense derived from the Cartesian doubt, but Husserl is insistent in pointing out that it is essentially different: to doubt reality, be it only methodically, is to take a position with regard to reality, and this Husserl will not do; reality simply does not enter into the question of *what* things are.

Once the epoche is put into operation it is never retracted. Here

9. Unfortunately in the whole discussion of contingency and necessity there enters in a strange mingling of metaphysics, epistemology, and logic — reminiscent of Plato in his earlier dialogues. It is true, by definition, that what might possibly not be is contingent, but it does not follow from this that what can be *thought of* as not being is contingent. Even less does it follow that the *knowledge* one has of such a being must be contingent. Quite obviously a knowledge which has as its object only "essences" cannot be contingent, but, by the same token, such a "knowledge" can very well be arbitrary, since these "essences" need not correspond to anything other than themselves — a point which Kant realized very well. Constancy of experience may strengthen the presumption of objective validity; it can scarcely remove arbitrariness entirely.

10. Though he never mentions Husserl directly, it is fairly clear that Husserl is among those Heidegger has in mind when he speaks of those who are concerned exclusively with "that which is" (*das Seiende*) and not at all with "being" (*das Sein*). See *supra*, Chap. 2, p. 39, n. 42.

again we see a difference between it and the Cartesian doubt, whose purpose is ultimately to eliminate itself in gaining certitude regarding what is doubted. On the contrary, the whole of phenomenology is carried out in a framework in which the epoche is constantly operative. The reason for this is precisely that the epoche itself serves to eliminate doubt because it eliminates all those elements which make doubt possible; they cannot be reintroduced except at the risk of reintroducing doubt. This is but another way of saying that it eliminates all those elements which are not essential and therefore necessary; with the epoche in operation, whatever is known is known as essential and necessary.

Since the epoche is negative, however, it functions as a *condition* for a knowledge of essences, not as a positive factor in grasping essences as they are; it simply assures that no foreign elements shall be admitted into the analysis; it says nothing positive with regard to what is there. If the phenomenological investigation is to be fruitful, the epoche must have its positive counterpart. This it has in the various levels of "reduction," on which is exploited the positive residue left after the epoche has been accomplished. In no sense of the word is the *reduction* to be looked on as a *deduction*; rather, in the constant application of the epoche, it is the gradual penetration into the purified essential residue, gradually revealing the pure subjectivity as the exclusive source of all objectivity. In Husserl's opinion the danger of a return to pure subjectivism in this process has been eliminated by the very fact that the essence of subjectivity has been found in an investigation where the subject itself has been reduced to phenomenality. It is here, in fact, that Husserl finds Descartes falling into his first error, which is to *conclude* from the *cogito* to the existence of a substantial subject: whereas, if Descartes had confined himself to the data of consciousness, he would have found *in* the *cogito* only the essence of subjectivity.[11]

One of the difficulties involved in understanding the work of Husserl as a whole is to be found precisely in this notion of reduction to pure subjectivity. In no one place does Husserl indicate the

11. Cf. *Cartesianische Meditationen,* pp. 202, 204; *Die Krisis der europäischen Wissenschaften* (The Hague: Martinus Nijhoff, 1954), p. 82.

whole process, and yet the important element of subjectivity can be understood, only if we realize that there are at least six levels of reduction, on each of which we have a subject of greater purity; and only when the subject is at its greatest purity do we have the strict science of phenomenology as Husserl understands it. It is only when the subject has been purified to the extent of being absolutely pure subjectivity that it can be the universal a priori source of objectivity.[12] And yet, we have to go through all of Husserl's works, published and unpublished, in order to discover just what the six levels of reduction are. The six levels, we might say, are six stages in seeing the implications of the original radical epoche. The first of these, which we can call the psychological reduction, is concerned with the phenomenon of consciousness itself and with its idealization. It is first in more ways than one: not only is it fundamental to all further progress in phenomenological investigation, leading as it does to an intuition of the very essence of that consciousness whose data are to be the sole source of information in the investigation of all being; it is also historically the first step taken by Husserl in his struggle against the psychologism of his day. Without naming it he had used it in the *Prolegomena to Pure Logic*, wherein he spoke out violently against the naturalization of consciousness and of ideas. Only, says Husserl, if the essence of consciousness can be disengaged from its factual concretizations, can we escape the relativism inherent in the multiplicity of contingent subjects, each of which has its own experiences, without being capable of guaranteeing that its experiences have any universal validity.[13] A multiplicity of subjects makes for a multiplicity of opinions, and a multiplicity of opinions makes for doubt.[14] Only the unity of a sort of Platonic form of consciousness makes for the elimination of doubt.[15]

The second reduction, known as the eidetic reduction, has as its

---

12. Here the relation of necessity and objectivity becomes extremely important. If the subject can *see* that things *cannot* be otherwise, it has guaranteed the objectivity of its own grasp of things.

13. So long as the appeal is primarily to logic, one wonders if this guarantee can ever be had.

14. Precisely Descartes' problem.

15. Where the data of consciousness are all that have to be considered.

aim the idealization of objectivity. This, too, was in operation as early as the *Logical Investigations*,[16] wherein Husserl had not yet developed either a theory of the epoche or of the reductions. Though this second reduction looks to objectivity it, too, is a stage in the gradual purification of subjectivity, since it looks at consciousness precisely insofar as its essence is to be consciousness-of something, thus purifying not only its "operation," which is not psychological activity, but also the term of that operation which is the object precisely as immanent in consciousness. We might say that the first reduction purifies the *cogito,* whereas the second reduction purifies the *cogitatum.* It is here that we begin to see the new notion of "immanent" — not too different from the scholastic notion — which was to characterize the ultimate identification, in Husserl's transcendental phenomenology, of subjectivity and objectivity.[17] Husserl could not conceive of ideas existing somewhere apart, nor could he conceive of them as being mere functions of a physical subject, *à la* Locke, Mill, or Hume. They had to have a being all their own, and this they have as immanent, objective terms of pure consciousness. Thus, we see that this reduction is quite obviously important, since it permits the extension of the phenomenological method to the objects of empirical science and also because it provides the basis for the next fundamental technique in the method, which is the technique of "ideation."

The remaining reductions are somewhat less easy to distinguish clearly, and there is even a faint suggestion of arbitrariness in their division. It may be that Husserl considered them not so much distinct steps in a reductive *process* as concomitant factors in a total framework of purification, wherein the "essential intuition" is rendered on the one hand purely *intuitive* and on the other purely *essential.* The first of these further reductions is termed by Husserl somewhat generically the "phenomenological reduction," which

16. Cf. *Logische Untersuchungen,* II, Investigation V, pp. 400–415.

17. Husserl accuses the psychologists of his day of seeing immanence only in terms of subjective *functions* and not at all in terms of their objective correlates. Cf. *Philosophie als strenge Wissenschaft,* pp. 315–16; *Logische Untersuchungen,* II, Investigation V, Nos. 16–21, pp. 397–425.

is to have as its result a subject which is in no sense of the term *objectified*: hence a "pure" subject. It is not easy to conceive of an awareness which in no way objectifies that of which it is an awareness, but unless we can do this we shall have missed the sense of Husserl's "phenomenological reduction." We might understand it as a *way* of grasping objects: in every intentional act an object is *given* by the very fact that the act is intentional; the object is that *of which* consciousness is consciousness. There can, then, be no consciousness-of a pure subject; that would be to objectify it and thus make it cease to be "pure." Still, "object" is an essentially relative term; there can be no object which is not object *for* a subject. Hence, if an object is genuinely *given* as object, it is given as object for a subject, and thus the subject, too, is given; it is a datum of consciousness. Just as there is no consciousness (act of consciousness) without its objective reference, so there can be no object without its subjective reference. So long as the term of this reference is not objectified it is "pure subject." [18] The difficulty is not insuperable, but since to speak *about* such a pure subject is to objectify it, Husserl is forced to approach the whole thing somewhat negatively, hoping that we shall understand the "residue" in terms of what has been eliminated from the consideration. [19]

If, then, there is a subject which is in no way an object, it is a subject of which we cannot be conscious in the strict sense of the term, since the very preposition "of" would indicate in it an objective relationship. And still we must say of this subject that it is known; in fact, it is the first absolute certitude. It is known and it is known in consciousness, but it is not known as that *of* which one is conscious; it is simply known as that which [20] is conscious, which is to say, as the subjective term of the act of consciousness, corre-

18. Small wonder that for Sartre such a consciousness, which borrows whatever intelligible being it has from the object *of which* it is consciousness, should be looked upon as the *néant*, and that its action should be a *néantisation* (cf. *supra*, Chap. 2, p. 37, n. 38).

19. Somewhat as "non-being" can be understood only in terms of the "being" which it negates.

20. Once again *language* proves inadequate. Strictly speaking a pure subject is not a *that which* at all.

sponding to the pure grammatical subject of the *cogito*. If the subject is at all conscious of being conscious it is conscious of itself as subject. It is of this subject that Husserl asserts so vigorously that it is not a substantial subject, not the subject, of a *sum* inferred from the *cogito,* but simply the subject of which I am immediately aware in being aware of the *cogito*.[21]

This subject, however, which precisely as subject is the very contradictory of an object *can* subsequently be objectified, in the sense that it can, as this subject, be deliberately made the object of reflection. In thus making it an object, according to Husserl, we can know it better, we can arrive at a knowledge of its essence, which is subjectivity as such.[22] We can, however, arrive at this pure subjectivity only as the result of another reduction, though it is admittedly very difficult to see how this further step is anything but a sort of abstraction, whereby the subject attained in the former reduction is universalized by being objectivated. Nor is it easy to see how this pure subjectivity differs from the abstract subjectivity of Kant, by which Husserl on his own admission was very much impressed. One is tempted to see in it little more than a transition from the pure subject to the pure transcendental ego, which is the term of the next reduction. Knowing that he had to arrive at the term of a pure transcendental ego, Husserl takes this somewhat obscure means of arriving; the step is dictated by the goal. In his earlier writings, in fact, Husserl scarcely makes the distinction. It would seem to have been necessitated by some kind of unexplained identification of essential knowledge and objective knowledge — a logical consequence of Husserl's phenomenological position.

The next reduction, which terminates in the pure transcendental ego, is, on the other hand, extremely important in distinguishing the phenomenology of Husserl from other forms of phenomenology, even from that of many of Husserl's disciples, who refuse to

21. *Formale und transzendentale Logik,* pp. 202–204; *Cartesianische Meditationen,* No. 13; *Krisis der europäischen Wissenschaften,* p. 82.

22. Since to speak of essence is to speak of ultimate *intelligibility,* it is difficult to see how the purely non-objective subject can have an essence at all. Or, is it accorded an essence in being objectified?

54

follow him this far.[23] Having resolutely refused to accept anything but the data of consciousness, and having just as resolutely refused to *infer* anything from the data of consciousness, Husserl could seem to be left with an intentionality which is an objective relation and nothing more. In the theory of his former teacher Brentano, in fact, intentionality is that and only that, with the addition that, for Brentano, its term is eminently real since as term it is that which exists outside consciousness and independently of consciousness, a reality to which consciousness is intentionally related. But to Husserl neither this realism of Brentano, which contradicts the pure immanence of strict science, nor the subjectivism of the psychologists, which rejects the objective validity for which he strives, are acceptable. For him an intention is not merely a mental relation; instead it is an ideal immanent term of consciousness. By the very fact that consciousness itself has been idealized in the way we have seen, its term, too, must be idealized. The result is an immanent object which is not the reproduction of an existing object (which would require an unprovable relation of causality between object and consciousness); nor is it a term projected, as it were, by consciousness. Rather it is a term "constituted" *in* consciousness.

That such a "constitution" should be not a production, not a reproduction, not a discovery may well seem difficult to grasp, but Husserl maintained this interpretation from 1922, when he first introduced it, to the very end of his life.[24] Now, it is precisely this "constitution" which is the transcendental function of subjectivity. To know a subjectivity which has this sort of function is to know one which is transcendentally related to the objects which are its intentions. That this relation is wholly enclosed within the immanent sphere of intentionality causes Husserl no difficulty at all. Since there is no objectivity which is not intentional, to know intentions is to know objectivity. This, of course, is not enough: there is only intentionality to be known, but it must be penetrated thoroughly,

23. E.g., Scheler, von Hildebrand, Merleau-Ponty, Ricoeur, Conrad-Martius.

24. It is, of course, present in germ as far back as *Die Idee der Phänomenologie*, written in 1907. The kind of "intuition" he there demands cannot logically be other than "constitutive."

if the result is to merit the title "knowledge." It is just this thorough, penetrating grasp of intentionality which is knowledge of the transcendental ego; knowing the transcendental ego we know objectivity; there is no other way of knowing it. The rest of phenomenology is but an explicitation of this. One knows an object in knowing the subject because to know a subject is to know it as essentially having a determined object. This transcendental subject, then, is the a priori source of objectivity; not only of the formal objectivity of reason, as it is for Kant, but also of the objectivity of experience, since ultimately that only can be an object which is constituted in the transcendental ego, the source of that intentionality without which there are no objects.

One would think that, having arrived at such a transcendental subject, one could advance no further on the path of reduction. Such is, in fact, the conclusion one seems forced to draw in reading only Husserl's published works. Even in the published work, however, and particularly in *Formal and Transcendental Logic* and in the *Cartesian Meditations,* Husserl has taken cognizance of the role of temporality in the constitution of the transcendental subject itself.[25] The subject is the a priori source of all objectivity, but it is not an unchanging source. Precisely as subject it has a history of its own, in which every object to which it is as subject related somehow enriches it, so that as subject it is constantly developing. The subject is not simply there as subject; it must be progressively constituted as subject. Such a subjective constitution cannot be static, since it is necessarily enriched by successive experiences, nor can it ever terminate in a subject which is simply the sum-total of all objective relations, since the cessation of dynamic constitution would also be the cessation of subjectivity.[26] The transcendental ego, then, becomes, as the term of this so-to-speak final reduction,

25. That Husserl was hesitant in speaking of a constitution which is not constitution of an object is not to be wondered at; the very "essence" of constitution would seem to need revision in order to make this possible.

26. This is the closest Husserl ever came to a phenomenology in the Hegelian sense. Since he resolutely refused a genuine dialectic, it is doubtful that he could have come any closer. By the same token, it remains doubtful whether his subject is ever genuinely historical.

a "pure flow of consciousness." Clearly, this is, in a certain sense, a return to the term of the first reduction, with the addition that it takes cognizance of the temporality of consciousness.[27] This temporalized subject is, in fact, extremely important for an understanding of Husserl's whole theory of constitution, though no one can pretend that the theory, even with this addition, is particularly clear. This much, however, it does make clear: constitution is not a sort of activation of innate intentions in consciousness. Consciousness grows, not because it gradually brings out that which was always present within it, but because with each experience the subject is more than it was before, and, since experience is a constant flow, the transcendental subject is constantly developing. It is, of course, the a priori source of all objectivity, but in the very constituting of objectivity it follows an order, and this order is its history. Thus, our analysis of the reductions has shown us that constitution is not meant by Husserl to be either a "discovery" of objectivity or a "creation" of objectivity out of whole cloth, so to speak; nor is it, finally, an "activating" of innate but latent intentions. We might well ask, of course, what is left, but for the present we shall have to be content with saying what it is not.[28]

It has unfortunately been necessary, in thus describing the six levels of reduction as found here and there in Husserl's writings, to go far beyond the point we had reached in our explanation thus far. There will, thus, be a certain overlapping, as we are compelled to go back and explain more fully some of the terms which have already been met with in this section. It is hoped that such a rapid summary of all the reductions will not cause too much confusion; to have taken the reductions one by one in the order in which they appear in Husserl's writing would unquestionably have been even more confusing. It has been necessary to spend this much time on the reductions, not only because they are so fundamental to the

---

27. Another reason for doubting that the reductions are six successive steps in a *process* of purification; they seem rather to be *elements* in a more and more thorough analysis of subjectivity.

28. Cf. Eugen Fink, "Die phänomenologische Philosophie Ed. Husserls in der gegenwärtigen Kritik," *Kantstudien*, XXXVIII (1933), 373.

whole of transcendental phenomenology, but also because an explanation of them is at the same time an explanation of much of the development in Husserl's original conception. Whether they make sense to us or not, we must admit that without the reductions the whole doctrine of intentionality is singularly sterile. Furthermore, if, as we said, phenomenology is a "science of essences," and if, according to Husserl, essences are necessarily ideal, before going on we must examine one more phenomenological technique, which is concerned precisely with grasping the essences of things as ideal. It is this technique, moreover, which in one way or another characterizes all those theories which go by the name of phenomenology, be they idealistic or realistic in their orientation. The technique in question is that of "ideation," and from it phenomenology derives its characterization as "descriptive," though, as we said, it might with even more accuracy be termed "meditative." Like the techniques already mentioned, it was practiced by Husserl long before he had developed a theory to justify it.

Remembering that phenomenology has only the data of consciousness with which to work and that its goal is a penetration to the "essences of things," we can understand that it must examine phenomena in such a way as to make them reveal the essences contained in them. The epoche and the reductions ensure that only phenomena will enter into the consideration, but of themselves they give no assurance that there will be a penetration of these phenomena to the very essences contained in them.[29] The process, then, of making essences stand out in consciousness begins with an "original" phenomenon, whether it be one of perception or of imagination. This original appearance serves merely as an "example" upon which the process of *ideation* can be built. The process itself consists in submitting the original perception or imagination to a series of "free" variations, wherein the object is viewed from various "aspects" (perceptual and imaginative). In this process of variations the possibilities are, so to speak, infinite, but it is not necessary to

---

29. It might be argued, of course, that the total reduction, properly understood, involves a complete penetration of essences. For the sake of exposition, however, ideation can be examined as a separate technique, and this Husserl himself does.

go through the infinite variety of possible aspects of the object; somewhere along the line it will be "seen" that there is an identical element underlying all variations, actual as well as possible. This identical element is the "sense" or essence of the object under investigation. Thus — and this has become characteristic of most phenomenological investigation — it is deemed possible to grasp the very essence of something after only one or a very few actual experiences of that which is in question.[30]

Lest there be doubt as to the justification for calling the result of this process the essence sought for, Husserl simply defines essence as that which remains identical in all possible variations of that which is being investigated. This also has the advantage of assuring the objective validity of the knowledge resulting from the process, since objective validity, too, is defined as the constant and universal identity of intention in an act of consciousness. Here again is one of the fundamental weaknesses of the phenomenological method, whether it be practiced by Husserl himself, by Max Scheler, by Dietrich von Hildebrand, or by Jean-Paul Sartre. Nor have the philosophers who draw their inspiration from Husserl sufficiently eliminated this precise weakness. What guarantee is there that the process of ideation as performed by one philosopher is necessarily more valid than that performed by another, precisely when the results of both are contradictory? However, the process does provide a strong basis for purely "internal" criticism of any phenomenological investigation: by using the same methods one can show that the "essence" arrived at is not justified by the process itself. Such a criticism, of course, can hardly be instituted except *within* the framework of the phenomenological method.

By this process, according to Husserl, there has been secured an answer to the problem raised by Kant of how to guarantee the objectivity of an act of cognition without appealing to anything outside the act of cognition itself. Rational knowledge is not to be

---

30. This would seem also to involve "seeing" that no additional variations could be significant in the investigation undertaken. This remains one of the most seriously questionable points in any merely phenomenological investigation — if, in fact, there be such.

verified by the criterion of an object assumed to exist outside the cognition of it, since what is outside cognition is by definition not known, and what is not known cannot be the criterion for knowledge; either reason is its own criterion, or reason has no criterion. As for Kant, so for Husserl, the validity of the act of cognition is contained in the very necessity of the act itself.[31] Husserl, however, finds this necessity in the constant identity of at least the "objective core" of the act, and this he does in accord with his theory of intentionality, which is precisely the immanent objectivity residing in consciousness. Where the objective element in an act of consciousness is constantly identical, it is necessary; and where it is necessary, its validity is guaranteed. This necessity, Husserl assures us, is not the psychological compulsion under which a subject is forced to see things in a certain way; rather, it is the logical necessity derived from the essences themselves. The distinction is, quite obviously, extremely fine, and it may well be doubtful whether anyone who has not already committed himself to phenomenology can clearly see the distinction at all. Eugen Fink, whom Husserl himself considered as one of his most authentic interpreters, claims that it is impossible to understand what phenomenology is without being oneself a phenomenologist.[32] That there can be a logical necessity which is more than the abstract necessity of formal rules of thought is the theme of *Formal and Transcendental Logic.* A transcendental logic contains the necessary laws of intentional constitution. Since this constitution is not a psychological process, the necessity imposed on objectivity by its laws is at once logical and ontological, but not psychological.[33]

How different this solution is in reality from that proposed by

---

31. Unfortunately this notion of necessity, which is not clarified, can refer to either logical or psychological necessity. Both Kant and Husserl *intend* that it should be the former, but one wonders if it is not just as frequently the latter.

32. "Die phänomenologische Philosophie Ed. Husserls," pp. 368–70; see *Cartesianische Meditationen*, critical remarks by Roman Ingarden, Appendix, p. 206 (not contained in the Cairns translation).

33. When all is said and done, it is questionable whether this necessity is really different from that imposed by Kant's a priori forms. This criticism does not, of course, invalidate Husserl's intuition, but it makes it a question as to whether Husserl was being quite so "scientific" as he claimed.

Kant is problematical. It is clear, at least, that as a solution to the problem of synthesizing reason and experience it is fundamentally Kantian in that it sees the necessary laws of reason as identical with the necessary laws of experience and, hence, ultimately with the necessary laws of phenomenal being. Since Husserl recognizes no noumenal being at all, these laws, then, become the necessary laws of the only being there is. Knowledge is not that act of consciousness which corresponds adequately with reality; rather, reality is that which is the object of the necessary act of consciousness called knowledge. We do not guarantee an act of knowledge by demonstrating that it corresponds with reality; we guarantee reality by demonstrating that it is the object of an act of knowledge. If we define knowledge as an act which has reality as its object, then if we prove that an act is one of knowledge we have thereby also proved that its object is real.[34] From this it is also clear that the subject of such knowledge cannot be simply the pure subject obtained as a result of the third reduction, since to a certain extent that subject is still individual and hence solipsistic. Husserl cannot be satisfied with simply asserting that what is found to be necessary for one subject is by that very fact necessary for any subject; if objective validity is to be universal, there must also be some sort of universality in the subject. Thus, the fourth reduction involves in itself the process of ideation, whereby the essence of subjectivity is seen and thus made the proper subject of necessary knowledge. As was said before, in discussing the fourth reduction, it is difficult to see that this subjectivity is anything but an abstraction and one might with reason hesitate to entrust the validation of objective knowledge to a mere abstraction.

Whether or not all this is justified, says Husserl, is not something which can be "proved," at least not in the ordinary acceptance of the term. Thus, the fourth fundamental technique of the phenomenological method is precisely the essential intuition, wherein the essence not only of "things" but also of events, of processes, of intuitions themselves are simply "seen." In order that this intuition be

34. Has Husserl really escaped from logical positivism?

definitive, one must not only "see" the essence of the object in question; one must also see that no one else can justifiably see it in any other way. Thus, as Max Scheler says, the phenomenologist could quite calmly accept the fact that the rest of the world disagreed with him; he would be absolutely sure simply on the basis of his own essential intuition; he would at the same time be sure that everyone else is wrong. This, of course, would be on the assumption — at least in Husserl's case — that historical, cultural, and social factors were not operative in "constituting" his "essential" intuition. No matter how arbitrary this intuition may seem, it should be clear that it is not conceived in the mind of the phenomenologist as simply an irrational leap beyond the data of experience. Rather it is intended as a rational penetration *into* the data of experience; and for this every element of the laborious process is necessary. Epoche, reductions, ideation, and essential intuition are not four successive techniques applied in an attempt to purify knowledge and thus render it certain. They are simply four interdependent factors in an over-all process known as "intentional constitution," which at one and the same time renders knowledge completely immanent and hence capable of complete verification, and completely necessary for subjectivity as such, which gives it its universal objective validity. The ultimate aim of all phenomenological method is an intuition of essence; but intuition is to be conceived not as a lyric leap into the unknown but rather as the term of a perfectly controlled process, which justifies itself from beginning to end.

In connection with this process it is significant that, for the majority of phenomenologists, history in the strict sense has little importance. This historical process through which thought has gone has no influence on its validity; the phenomenologist can "see" whether an idea is valid, whether or not he knows its history. Unfortunately, however, too many phenomenologists — and Husserl belongs to their number — do not seem to be sufficiently aware that their own history has actually determined the very intuitions they have. This lack of concern for history, of course, varies in degree, but to a greater or lesser extent all the phenomenologists who draw their inspiration from Husserl seem convinced that philosophy *could* begin with them, though they admit that men have been philosophizing for centuries, and that some of them have even come up with fairly good ideas. Thus, too, the phenomenologist is rarely concerned with the opinions of others, except perhaps to reject them when they disagree with his, or to accept them when they agree. One significant exception to this rule would be Gabriel Marcel, who carries his Platonism just a bit further than the rest and sees not only the intuition of essences but also dialogue as indispensable to philosophy. Thus, for Marcel, an individual intuition, even his own, has little significance by itself. Like other phenomenologists, he will appeal to appearances, but he does so on the *assumption* that other men have had and do have similar experiences.[35] On this basis it is possible by discussion to seek to persuade others to derive from these experiences the same intuitions which one has gained oneself. At the same time it is very possible that one will be brought to modify one's own "intuition" by contact with the "intuition" of others. The result may very well be a sort of "social" intuition, which has more validity precisely because man is more truly man when acting in accord with others.[36] Thus, the opinions of others, both in the past and in the present, are extremely important, since man thinks authentically as man only when he thinks in a framework which is both historical and social.[37]

It would, of course, be unfair to assert that all this is completely absent from the thought of Husserl. The source of all objectivity, it is true, is for Husserl the transcendental a priori subject, and in his early writings at least this subject is very much individual or, at best, somewhat abstractly multiple. Still, particularly in his later writing, Husserl recognized that the transcendental a priori subject was both concretely historical and concretely multiple. Thus, in theory, he recognized that there is a process which is not confined to the process within the individual consciousness, but which takes in the thought of many men. The difficulty, however, is that this

---

35. See *supra*, Chap. 2, p. 40, n. 46.

36. "Pure subjectivism is based on an illusion, since I am for myself only on condition that I am really contrasted to other persons." Gabriel Marcel in *Royce's Metaphysics*, trans. Virginia and Gordon Ringer (Chicago: Regnery, 1956) p. 103.

37. Another of the elements in Hegel's phenomenology which seems to have escaped Husserl.

theory seems to have had very little concrete effect on Husserl's own thought. He admitted in the abstract that thought has followed a process, but in the concrete he seems to have had little concern for what this process actually was and is. Husserl had little patience with disagreement, and, except in rare instances, seems to have profited little by discussion or criticism.

It has seemed necessary to make these few remarks on Husserl's comparative isolation from the historical stream of thought before entering more in detail into the further development of his own phenomenological theory.

4

THEORY OF COGNITION AS THEORY OF BEING

IT SHOULD BY THIS TIME BE CLEAR that the phenomenological method as developed by Husserl is a far cry from its early characterization as a "descriptive psychology"; it is far more concerned with the essence of *thought* than with a description of *thinking*. Nevertheless, transcendental phenomenology, even in its most developed form, remains essentially tributary to the new conception of psychology which grew out of the first halting steps taken in the *Philosophy of Arithmetic* and the first edition of the *Logical Investigations*. From these early attempts was developed the notion of consciousness upon which the whole of phenomenology continues to depend. It is this notion of consciousness, with its essential intentionality, which enabled Husserl to reveal the profound character of the *cogito* as he saw it: no longer evidence for the existence of a substantial *ego,* as it was for Descartes, but rather evidence that the very being of the *ego* is conscious being,[1] which is but another way of saying that the being of the *ego* is to be subject.[2] Descartes had so effectively separated subject and object that, like Humpty-Dumpty, they seem destined never to be brought together again. It is as though Husserl were reaching out beyond materialism, beyond

1. Once again we see the difficulty of translating the German *Bewusstsein*. When an object is grasped, it is *bewusst*; and when a subject is conscious, it is *bewusst*. Hence, the kind of being expressed by *Bewusstsein* can be both objective and subjective. The being whereby the object is known and the subject is conscious is, then, the same.

2. Many of the manuscripts preserved at Louvain reveal that, in later years, Husserl was much bothered by the problems of birth, death, and sleep. If subject is constituted as subject by consciousness, what happens when there is no consciousness? Can subject begin to be and cease to be? Can the reduction really prescind from such questions? If not, is there an element of contingency, even in conscious being?

65

German idealism (to which he owed much), beyond Kantian criticism, beyond English empiricism, beyond Descartes himself to a scholasticism which saw real being and mental being as two modes of the same being — in German, *Sein* and *Bewusst-sein*. The difference is that, without being quite aware of his debt to history, Husserl has been affected by all the intervening philosophizing which had been touched off by Descartes. There is, after all, a very true sense in which subjectivity is responsible for objectivity; not in the sense that a subject *creates* its own object, but in the sense that an object is an object only because it is related to a subject. Conversely, of course, a subject is a subject only because it is related to an object; but Husserl was by no means unaware of this. He did not try to bring subject and object together again; he simply refused to admit that they ever could be separated, since each is utterly meaningless except in reference to the other. Had Husserl really read Hegel he could not fail to have been far less violent in his condemnation of his predecessor, since like Hegel he was trying to point out that the terms of the subject–object relationship are intelligible only through each other.

If, then, one can justifiably refuse to separate subject and object, it would seem that the cognitive relationship is not really a relationship. If the being of subject as subject is identical with the being of object as object,[3] then an absolute guarantee of one is an absolute guarantee of the other. Now, a being which is absolutely guaranteed can be called absolute being, because its being is absolutely necessary. It is this sort of absolute being which Husserl had been seeking since the beginning of his career, a quest which he expressed so eloquently in the article "Philosophy as Rigorous Science." In discovering pure transcendental subjectivity, Husserl felt that he had attained the object of his quest, though he was well aware that not all problems were thereby solved. The solution to the remaining problems, however, was at hand, he felt, if the implications of pure transcendental subjectivity could be fully exploited. If all knowledge could be guaranteed by recourse to transcendental subjectivity, then the universal a priori science he sought was a fact, even

3. One is reminded of the scholastic *intellectus in actu est intellectum in actu*.

66

though explicitating its implications might be the work of generations (or centuries) for scholars applying the phenomenological
method.[4]

The quest for an absolute is certainly not new in philosophy; it
is in fact the notion of an absolute which weaves the guiding thread
throughout so many and diverse philosophies, from Plato to Martin
Heidegger. We have but to look at Plato's efforts to discover a unified form of knowledge in the *Theaetetus* or his ascension to the
absolute Good beyond Being in the *Republic* to see the need which
philosophers have always felt somehow to gather the multiplicity
of experience into the unity of reason. It was Aristotle's problem;
it was Plotinus' problem; it was Augustine's. We see it dominating
the thought of the scholastics; we find it alive in Descartes, in Kant,
and in Hegel. With the dawn of modern philosophy, however,
the notion of the absolute takes on a new coloration; absolute being
becomes the being of which subjects can be absolutely certain. And
here, in a certain sense, comes the great cleavage — between those
who feel that such an absolute certitude is attainable and those who
feel either that it is utterly unattainable or that it is attainable only
by relinquishing all ambition to attain an absolute in knowledge
which will also be a metaphysical absolute. Among the latter might
be numbered those existentialists who feel that a metaphysical absolute can be *approached,* but not by rational means.

Husserl belongs quite definitely to the number of those who feel
that an absolute knowledge is attainable — he passionately rejects
all skepticism — and he is convinced that this absolute is a metaphysical absolute,[5] although he rejects equally passionately any
"thing-in-itself" metaphysics as illusory. Thus, for Husserl there is
simply an identification between the being of which one is absolutely certain and absolute being, since for him any other absolute

4. Cf. *Philosophie als strenge Wissenschaft*, pp. 333, 338. Husserl was accustomed
to assign to his students subjects for phenomenological analysis, somewhat as a
professor of natural science would assign experiments in the laboratory. Many of
these analyses appeared later in the *Jahrbuch für Philosophie und phänomenologische Forschung,* under Husserl's direction.

5. In the sense that the only "being" he will recognize as worthy of the title is
being-in-consciousness, which is absolute because absolutely incontrovertible.

would be meaningless. Now, a being of which one is absolutely certain is one which admits of no doubt; and doubt, according to Husserl, can be eliminated only if every possible source of doubt has been eliminated. This, as we have seen, he feels has been eliminated by eliminating from knowledge all elements which can in any way be considered extraneous to consciousness. Thus, if there is an absolute being, it must be the being which is in consciousness.

Only fairly late in his career did Husserl realize that a being in consciousness which in no way *depends*[6] on any element extraneous to consciousness must be a being *constituted* in consciousness itself. Obviously a being so constituted is not absolute by the very fact that it is so constituted; there must be an absolute *mode* of constitution, and that will ultimately be a constitution which carries with it an absolute necessity. Since such a necessity would be utterly meaningless for Husserl were it to be anything but subjective, and since it would have no determinable validity were it not objective, the last years of Husserl's life were completely filled with the endeavor to identify subjective and objective necessity. Thus, his philosophy which begins as a theory of cognition also ends as a theory of cognition,[7] in which the term of absolute knowledge is identified with absolute being. Such an identification was rendered possible by a consistent application of his theory of intentionality; and this theory was rendered consistent by a theory of "intentional constitution," which ultimately rejoins Kant in its final conviction that the source of all necessity is *reason*. Nor is the end result of all this as different from the conviction of Kant as Husserl would like to persuade himself. According to Kant, pure reason could attain to absolute knowledge, provided it limit itself to phenomena and

6. To depend on what is extraneous to consciousness is to depend on what is essentially contingent and, hence, to be doubtful. Unless, of course, there be a metaphysical absolute, *à la* Hegel, which Husserl simply refuses to consider. Even the *veracitas Dei* of Descartes is for Husserl simply Descartes' lack of fidelity to his own rational principles. Cf. *Erste Philosophie (1923/24)*, I, ed. Rudolf Boehm (The Hague: Martinus Nijhoff, 1956) 65–66.

7. This constitutes the theme of a remarkable book by Emmanuel Lévinas, *La théorie de l'intuition dans la phénoménologie de Husserl* (Paris: Alcan, 1930). The book is all the more remarkable in that it was written at a time when very little was known of Husserl outside Germany.

either leave the nonphenomenal (God, freedom, immortality) to practical reason or be satisfied to accept a being of which one can think but which one cannot know. Husserl, too, will say that pure reason can attain to absolute knowledge, but he sees no need of limiting this; what may be outside the scope of pure reason he simply will not dignify with the title "being," with the result that it is not possible even to think of a being which cannot be known — what cannot be known rationally is not being.[8] Husserl does not limit reason; he limits being. One must judge for oneself whether, in the last analysis, he has really said anything different from Kant, or whether he has said the same thing in a different way.

One thing, however, is sure: by virtue of his theory of intentionality, Husserl is quite convinced that he has said something different from Kant. By returning to Descartes — a Descartes whom he misread somewhat — Husserl will constitute a true *mathesis universalis,* wherein the whole of being can be rationalized. The whole of being can be thus rationalized, because the whole of being can be reduced to what is "intentionally constituted" in reason. Husserl never seems to have been aware that by identifying being and that which is intentionally constituted he had simply skirted the whole problem. Nor does he seem to have been aware that, since consciousness itself is not constituted, his own principles lead to the conclusion of Sartre, according to whom consciousness must be the contradictory of being, which is to say, nonbeing.[9] On the other hand, those disciples of Husserl who have refused his theory of intentional constitution in all its radicality do not seem to realize that they have reintroduced into their investigations all the contingency and arbitrariness which Husserl was at such pains to eliminate — if indeed they have not objectified subjectivity to an extent which even Husserl did not.

8. This results in what most thinkers have considered a contradiction: a knowledge which is at one and the same time "intuitional" and "rational."

9. Husserl did, of course, in the Fourth Cartesian Meditation and in *Ideen II,* ed. Walter Biemel (The Hague: Martinus Nijhoff, 1925), treat the question of subjective constitution, but the suspicion remains that, since it is but the converse of objective constitution, its result is but the opposite of objective being — or non-being, in the sense in which Sartre understands it.

Before going any further into the details of Husserl's "universal phenomenology of reason," however, we should examine the steps which led him to think that such a complete rationalization of being was possible. Obviously it can be done, only if it is possible to rationalize experience, which is recognized by all in one form or another as our only *immediate* contact with being.

It is something of a mystery that the concept of a subjectivity which is constitutive of objectivity should have been developed so late in the thought of Husserl. One can almost excuse the critics who do not understand Husserl's elaborations regarding the transcendental subjectivity, since Husserl himself seems for so many years to have ignored the fact that a theory of intentional constitution was inevitable, if his entire theory was to be consistent. A rationalization of knowledge which was to be both more thoroughgoing and more universal than Kant's could not afford to admit of any elements in the cognitive synthesis which would not be a priori. The identification which we have made between his theory of cognition and his theory of being had already been tacitly enunciated at the very beginning in the axiom he employed so often, "to things themselves!" Through this axiom he was demanding that every investigation of being be a return to the very source of being and of knowledge. But until he had made clear to himself what this source had to be, in a theory which accepted only the immanent data of consciousness, it is not unreasonable to expect that his whole theory would be misunderstood.

As we saw, the *Logical Investigations* were intended as a critique of cognition, but they succeeded only in presenting a critique of meaning, which meaning could not be verified except when fulfilled in intuition. What was obscure at this time was precisely what this intuition was supposed to be. Though there are in the *Logical Investigations* vague allusions to an intuition which is itself intentional, it was not until the *Formal and Transcendental Logic* — written twenty-nine years after the first edition of the *Logical Investigations* — that the concept of intentionality as an "operation" of consciousness itself becomes clear enough to enable us to understand that intuition is to be looked on as a constitutive function of consciousness and hence of the subjectivity itself.[10] Up to that time one had the impression that there were, so to speak, two acts of consciousness, one the simple intention, which carried with it an "empty" meaning, and the other an intuition whereby the meaning contained in the simple intention was justified or validated. But, if intuition were only that, it would not be too much different from a realistic form of experience, with which all forms of rationality must be constantly continuous, if they are to have any objective justification. For Husserl to have done this would have been to leave the dilemma of reason and experience exactly where he found it. Nor could he be satisfied with a Kantian intuition, which was *formally a priori,* it is true, but operative only on the level of sensibility and confined to the very general forms of space and time. Still, it is not until the *Formal and Transcendental Logic* that we find really clear indications in Husserl's writing that he looked upon intuition itself as an operation of the subjectivity, and that the synthesis whereby a mere intention becomes a verified intention was to be accomplished entirely within the immanent sphere of consciousness itself.

Now, in a theory of pure intentionality such as Husserl's, intuition simply cannot be limited, as it is in the work of Kant, to sensible intuition. Rather, Husserl defines intuition as "original consciousness," [11] which means any act of consciousness in which an object is "given in itself" has its *origin* precisely as an object. Nor does this "given in itself" mean given independently of the very operation[12] of consciousness. An object of intuition is given in itself, precisely because it is intuition which constitutes it as the veritable object of consciousness. Thus, being in consciousness (*Bewusst-sein*) is veritable being, not merely because it is constituted, but because it is constituted in a very special way, which is to say, in the manner of intuition, a mode of intending which

10. It is difficult to give "subjectivity" any content save that of a sum total of conscious acts, noetically considered. Husserl, however, was averse to simplifying it to such an extent.

11. It might even be better to coin a word in English and call it "originary consciousness."

12. Intentional, not psychological, "operation."

can be determined simply by examining the intentional act it-self.[13]

Here is the point at which Husserl does differ from Kant. According to Kant there are in every cognition two elements: the one material, the other formal. The material element is contributed by experience, or sensible intuition; the formal element is contributed by the operation of consciousness, or the subjectivity. Thus, there is a certain independence of the two elements; over the material element the consciousness properly so called has no control, it is simply "given," whereas over the formal element it has complete control. The formal, then, is the a priori element in cognition, since from it and it alone does cognition derive the necessity whereby it can be termed knowledge. Thus, there is knowledge strictly speaking only on the formal level; the material level is, so to speak, but the occasion which sets the autonomous a priori of the formal level in operation. But for Husserl, to speak only of a formal a priori would be to leave knowledge still with a certain element of contingency, which would be precisely that element contributed by something which is not consciousness itself. A merely formal a priori would be nothing more than a sort of projection of necessity upon that over which consciousness had no control and would, hence, give no assurance of *objective* validity. For his project of a thoroughgoing and universal science of being this could not be sufficient, since it would attribute some sort of being to that which eternally escapes reason and, hence, science. A complete science of being is possible only on condition that there be possible a complete rationalization of knowledge, which is to say, an apriorization not only of reason but also of experience. He would make experience itself, or the intuitional element in cognition, an "operation" of the subjectivity. Thus, for Husserl, intuition is not something upon which reason can work in order to transform it into necessary knowledge; it is ultimately a function of reason itself.[14] Rightly understood experience, too, is an operation

13. One cannot "prove" that an intuition is an intuition; one simply "sees" it.
14. This theory of intuition had been adumbrated in *Ideen I*, but not made explicit until *Formale und transzendentale Logik* (it is what makes logic tran-

of reason, having its own laws and its own necessities. The data of intuition are not to be taken and transformed, they are to be constituted, precisely as data of intuition.[15] The reality of being is, for Husserl, its objective presence to consciousness. Such an objective presence, however, can be guaranteed only if it is immediate, a "presence-in-itself." Now, it has always been admitted that only in experience can objects be immediately present. Hence, Husserl is forced to say that being in the full sense is an objective correlate of experience. Intuition and experience, then, can be identified, but for Husserl this does not mean that intuition is confined to sensibility; rather it means that experience is broadened to take in the intellectual, the intuitions whereby essences are grasped. When we add to this the conviction that all genuine intuition is constitutive of its object, we have an immediate presence to consciousness which is at the same time an a priori grasp of the object in question. With this it is possible to say that every element in the cognitive synthesis is a priori and, hence, rational in the sense in which Husserl understands the term.

Thus, though Husserl agrees with Kant in recognizing that thought without experience is but an empty shell, he is convinced that Kant drew a false conclusion from this elementary law of cognition. According to Husserl, Kant simply did not face courageously the fact of experience; he accepted it as though it were a fact belonging to a different level from that of a priori cognition. Thus, says Husserl, Kant could not completely rationalize knowledge since he felt forced to posit some sort of "irrational X," a "thing-in-itself," precisely at the point where consciousness should come into contact with objectivity.[16] Had he, on the other hand, recognized the constitutive function of intentionality which permits

scendental). It is not, however, until the Third Cartesian Meditation that the theory becomes fully explicit.

15. For Kant, transcendental cognition is precisely *not* experience; cf. *Kritik der reinen Vernunft,* pp. 98–99. For Husserl, experience itself must be transcendental — whence the difference between a merely formal a priori and an a priori which is both formal and material.

16. Cf. *Formale und transzendentale Logik,* pp. 227–34.

us to conceive at one and the same time intuition as rational and reason as intuitional, he would not have stopped short before the ideal of complete rationality — complete rationalization of knowledge and complete rationalization of being. Had he recognized not only a formal but also a material a priori, he would have seen the possibility of rationalizing original consciousness, which is to say, the first and fundamental contact with objectivity, which is experience.

Whether or not one agrees with Husserl's interpretation of Kant — and it is admittedly superficial — one cannot fail to be struck by the boldness of Husserl's solution to the problem of integral rationality. It is, in fact, this radical effort at complete rationalization which makes Husserl's entire life work so thoroughly programmatic. His repeated insistence upon a return to experience is not merely a desire to achieve direct contact with objectivity rather than with its symbols; it is rather an insistent demand on a validation of experience itself, without which any further cognition can be only imperfectly rational. In this sense no philosopher has ever been so thoroughly rationalistic as Husserl. From this point of view the whole of phenomenology can be characterized by an expression which cannot but seem strange to the whole tradition which sees in the relationship of reason and experience a paradox to be reconciled; phenomenology is described as a "logic of experience."[17] Experience, he is convinced, has its own laws, they are a priori laws, necessary laws, and they are discoverable by investigation. These laws are "discoverable" in an adequate investigation of subjectivity. Husserl will not, however, accept a subjectivity which merely *discovers* the essential laws of experience; rather he will insist upon a subjectivity wherein these essential laws are *constituted*.[18]

17. The expression is, it is true, used adjectively — "erfahrungslogischem Bewusstsein" (*Philosophie als strenge Wissenschaft*, p. 299), "in erfahrungslogischem Vorgehen" (*ibid.*, p. 308). This is what he will later call a "pre-predicative logic" (*Erfahrung und Urteil*, No. 7; *Formale und transzendentale Logik*, No. 86). The same concept is expressed by "the a priori of experience," "experimental reason," or "pre-predicative reason."

18. As in the case of "subjective constitution," the notion of constitution here

Husserl's *Formal and Transcendental Logic,* published in 1929, is significant not only as a renewed effort to validate logical concepts, but more as a sustained attempt to examine the laws which govern not only the form but also the content of judgment. Nor is it merely a material logic, in the sense of a logic which seeks to determine the truth of judgments, as opposed to their mere correctness, although it is also that; rather, it is a logic which seeks to examine into the content of judgment and to determine the general rules governing any judgment whose content is true. To such a logic, quite obviously, a theory of evidence is indispensable, since evidence is the criterion whereby the content of a judgment can be evaluated. In Husserl's opinion, however, it would be an error to look upon evidence as being primarily a criterion of truth, a measuring rod, so to speak, permitting us to say whether a proposition is true or not. Rather, says he, evidence is concerned primarily not with truth at all but with objectivity and consequently with being; it is being's state of being clearly seen.[19]

Since there are varying degrees of clarity with which an object can be present to consciousness, it is not, according to Husserl, of the essence of evidence that it be apodictic. The highest form of evidence is apodictic and is hence the perfect guarantee of truth, but any object is evident so long as it is in itself present to consciousness, even though it be not present in such a way as to necessitate intellectual assent.[20] It was, in fact, the extreme desire to find a certitude, which would assure non-deception in judgment, to find an absolute criterion of judgment, which concealed

takes a peculiar twist. Because these laws, according to which objectivity is constituted in experience, are rooted in the essence of subjectivity, the laws themselves are said to be "constituted." Cf. *Formale und transzendentale Logik,* pp. 221–22; *Erfahrung und Urteil,* p. 50.

19. The notion of evidence has always caused trouble. As a least common denominator throughout the history of philosophy we might take the notion of that which neither *need* be nor *can* be proved, precisely because it is *seen* to be true.

20. Cf. *Cartesianische Meditationen,* p. 52; *Erfahrung und Urteil,* pp. 11–14; "Die Frage nach dem Ursprung der Geometrie als intentional-historisches Problem," *Revue internationale de Philosophie,* I (1938–39), 209.

from the logicians the real essence of evidence. To say that an object is evident is to say that it is "given"; and what is given neither can nor need be "proved." To say that it cannot be proved, however, is not to say that it cannot be rendered more perfectly given. There are various degrees of givenness, only the most perfect of which is apodictic evidence, wherein an object is given as absolutely necessary. Now, according to Husserl, an object can be given only in so far as it is constituted; its givenness is a function of intentional constitution. An object which is apodictically evident, then, which is given with absolute necessity, must be given in virtue of the constitutive function of reason, the only faculty of necessity.[21]

Thus, to understand evidence is to understand the different ways in which an object can be in itself present to consciousness. It can be present at all *only* as thus constituted by the operation of consciousness itself, and it can be present as necessary *only* as constituted by the highest operation of consciousness, which is reason. Once this has been accepted, the investigation of evidence becomes the investigation of consciousness in its constitutive functions, obviously a purely immanent investigation. And so, though Husserl agrees with Kant that only experience can give to judgment a content, he will enlarge the notion of experience to include any constitutive operation of consciousness, whereby an object is genuinely "given" to consciousness, as opposed to *merely* intended.[22] Since all operations of consciousness are subject to determinable a priori laws — and it is the function of phenomenology to determine them — the constitutive operations wherein objects are rendered really present are also subject to such laws; and the determination of these laws is a logic — not merely a formal

21. This is not particularly phenomenological; it is almost scholastic. If we begin by defining reason as *the* faculty of necessity, then quite obviously all necessity in cognition must be somehow a function of reason. No matter how true this may be, it has not been arrived at through an analysis of phenomena.

22. The opposition between "mere" or "empty" intention and intuition, introduced in the *Logische Untersuchungen,* is thus maintained to the end. With the theory of constitutive intentionality, however, the difference becomes more clearly one in the *manner* of intending.

logic — concerned with the laws governing *correct thinking,* but above all a transcendental logic concerned with the laws governing the way consciousness gives content to its thought. Such a logic will ultimately contain the laws governing the very being of objects as present to consciousness. It is precisely this second sort of logic which we can call a "logic of experience," since its laws govern those constitutive operations wherein objects are in varying degrees rendered really present to consciousness. By virtue of this logic, the "reconciliation" of reason and experience will ultimately be complete, since reason itself will be a kind of experience, and experience itself will be rationalizable.

Quite obviously experience will be rationalizable in this sense, only if it can be made completely a priori; and just as obviously it can be made completely a priori only if its content as well as its form can be subjected to necessary laws.[23] In a certain sense, of course, all this is very tautological, since law belongs to the immanent sphere alone, according to Husserl, and necessary laws belong to the sphere of reason alone; but it is imperative to show how he conceives the very possibility of a universal science of phenomenology. A universal science is one in which no element of the cognitive synthesis is not scientific, which is but another way of saying that no element of the cognitive synthesis can escape immanent validation. Now, if this be the case, experience can admit of absolutely nothing coming in, so to speak, from the outside. If experience has a rational explanation — and, according to Husserl, it must — then the explanation must be sought, and found, within the transcendental subjectivity. Nor does this mean *denying* that there is some sort of reality outside the subject; it simply means refusing to this sort of reality any *being,* since to be authentically is to be absolutely, and to be absolutely is to be for a subject, and to be for a subject is to be *constituted* in subjectivity itself.[24]

23. Something Kant would not attempt to do.
24. By some of his own followers, Husserl is accused of having made a "shift" to idealism with *Ideen I.* If, however, we examine closely the theory of intentionality as proposed in the *Logische Untersuchungen* and couple it with the ideal of strict scientific philosophy, we shall see that the present result was even then inevitable.

From the beginning to the end of his career, Husserl insisted that his theories had nothing in common with subjectivism, in the ordinary acceptance of that term. By making not only reason but also experience a constitutive function of transcendental subjectivity, it is true, he has made of the subject the complete source of knowledge. His contention was, however, that subjectivism in the strict sense is arbitrary and relativistic, and this, he claimed, constitutive phenomenology is not. A transcendental subjectivity, he says, is in no way arbitrary; it is rigidly controlled by the "laws" of its own operation. A constituted object can be neither arbitrary nor relative, because the laws which govern its constitution are necessary. In this way, he is convinced, *transcendental* experience is less subjective than would be a passive reception of impressions from without. The latter would be at the mercy of any coloration which an individual might give it; whereas the former is completely a priori and hence completely determined. Subjectivity "makes" neither objects nor laws; the ideal laws of constituted objectivity are there, and to disregard them is to abandon any claim to valid knowledge.[25]

The big problem of transcendental phenomenology is, of course, to explain *how* these laws are "there." In this, Husserl's position undergoes considerable development, without ever becoming completely satisfactory. That it never became *completely* satisfactory is understandable; nor should one make the mistake of simply looking on it as ridiculous, as Aristotle did, regarding Plato's teaching on "separated" forms. Husserl was too subtle a thinker to have meant by "ideal laws" what so many naïve interpretations thought he meant — the Aristotelian mentality is not calculated to understand sympathetically any position but its own. It has been said, not without justification, that Kant rediscovered Plato and reexpressed Plato's ideal forms in terms of subjectivity. It might, with equal justification, be said that Husserl rediscovered both Plato and Kant, seeking to express the positions of both in terms

25. For Husserl, as for Kant, and for the whole philosophy of the "Enlightenment," law seems to have had some mystic character. Thus, they miss the *abstract* character of law, based as it is on induction.

of constitutive intentionality. Plato saw essences as necessary and immutable; Kant strove to explain their necessity and immutability in terms of a formal subjective a priori; Husserl sought to achieve the same goal in a framework of formal *and* material a priori. Plato had recognized that, if there is necessity at all, it belongs to the ideal order. Kant has specified the ideal order as belonging exclusively to subjectivity and its necessity as attaching solely to the formalizing function of reason. Husserl sought to extend necessity from form to content, thus apriorizing the whole of knowledge — content as well as form.

Husserl was, of course, not the first philosopher to identify being and intelligibility. Nor was he the first to seek in subjectivity an explanation of intelligibility. It is difficult, however, to find a philosopher who identifies being and intelligibility as deliberately as does Husserl in making both depend on constitutive intentionality. According to this theory, not only is knowledge constituted in consciousness, but the very *being* of that which is known is so constituted; only absolute being is being in the full sense, and only being in consciousness (*Bewusst-sein*) is absolute being. Now, since being is in consciousness only as constituted, being is absolute only as constituted. Thus, intentional constitution has become a universal explanation or "clarification" of being.[26] "Nothing is, except by a proper *operation* of consciousness, *whether actual or potential*."[27] If, then, the task of philosophy is to understand being, its method must be to penetrate the subjectivity wherein being has its source. In this way Husserl derives an entire philosophy from what he calls a "radical consciousness of self."[28]

As we have pointed out before, however, the "self" of which one seeks a consciousness is not merely a substantial center of consciousness; it is a "transcendental" subject, whose very being is to be related to objects. Now, if we take the sum total of objects,

26. This term comes to the fore in *Ideen III,* ed. Walter Biemel (The Hague: Martinus Nijhoff, 1925), and in *Formale und transzendentale Logik* — both belonging to the same period in Husserl's development.

27. *Formale und transzendentale Logik,* p. 207.

28. Cf. the First Cartesian Meditation, "A Philosophical Examination of Conscience."

known or knowable, we have Husserl's notion of "the world"; and if we take the sum total of subjective relations to this world we have his notion of a "transcendental subjectivity." To know such a subjectivity adequately is to know the world to which it is related, which is to say, it is to know the whole of being. Never is this adequate knowledge of subjectivity more than an ideal — to be approached but not fully attained.[29] Still, only by aiming at it can we attain any authentic knowledge of being at all. And, what makes such a knowledge of being authentic is the fact that the very knowing of being constitutes being as what it is. It is for this reason that only a phenomenology of being can be a *science* of being; the gap between being and consciousness highlighted by Descartes can be bridged only if consciousness is constitutive of being. "Only a science transcendentally clarified and justified, in the phenomenological sense, can be the ultimate science. Only a world clarified by transcendental phenomenology can be a world definitively comprehended."[30] To put it another way: being is constituted as such by a relationship to transcendental subjectivity, and only when it is known as such is it known as it is. This, says Husserl, is not "subjectivizing" being; it is merely recognizing the only possibility for eliminating doubt in grasping it. The mathematician cannot doubt that a triangle has three sides; its being as a triangle is its being constituted as a figure having three sides. According to transcendental phenomenology, the being of anything is its being constituted as what it is.[31]

Once more we must call attention to Husserl's vigorous insistence that such constitution can never be arbitrary, precisely because the laws of constitution are inviolable. If, in an act of perception, a tree is constituted, it is a real tree which is perceived and not a telegraph pole. Were the object anything but a tree, the act would

29. Here again, Husserl seems to have had some inkling of the historical and social dimension of knowledge — a dimension which, unfortunately, he never adequately exploited.

30. *Formale und transzendentale Logik,* p. 14.

31. This is the very summit of essentialism. For Husserl, the reference to existence offers no problem; it simply has no significance for being. Thus, too, the philosopher is, in his eyes, a "disinterested spectator."

not be one of perception; the laws of constitution belonging to perception would have been violated. The difference, then, is not that, in becoming a transcendental phenomenologist and seeing all things as constituted in the transcendental subjectivity, one sees another world. One sees the same world, but one sees it minus those elements which could make one doubt what one sees; it is guaranteed as seen by the fact that the very seeing is an operation of consciousness, guaranteed by its conformity to the necessary laws of subjective constitution. If an act is in conformity with the laws of perception, it is an act of perception; and that is all there is to it. To understand the operation of consciousness is to understand its object, since a complete act of consciousness contains its object as it is. This, of course, is but a reiteration of the assertion that every act of consciousness is essentially intentional; to understand fully its intentionality is to understand its object. The knowledge which a subject has of its own experiences, and thereby of itself, is knowledge of a world, since experience is essentially experience-of, and the totality of experience is experience-of-this-world *of which* it is the experience. The phenomenologist seeks to penetrate more deeply into this world by penetrating more deeply into the experience of it. In so doing he does not seek to change it; he seeks rather to "clarify" it, to "guarantee" it, to "justify" it — and this he does by making it entirely *his*; that is, constituted as a world *for* him.

There may be still some doubt as to just how "objective" all this is. It is all very well to assert that a subjectivity following the necessary laws which govern it must constitute valid objectivity; but does the assertion make it true? Husserl was well aware that such doubts could still subsist. Consequently his attempts to guarantee the objectivity of phenomenology kept pace with his attempts to develop it as a more and more completely immanent discipline.

5

THE SENSE OF OBJECTIVITY

THE ONE WEAKNESS which phenomenology has never quite overcome is that which is contained in the very project of the *Logical Investigations*. They are for the most part concerned with an analysis of meaning; and, although this meaning is not looked upon as valid until it has been confirmed by an intuition of a necessary essence, the suspicion always remains that a meaning is what one *wants* it to be. Thus, the very essential investigations which constitute the major portion of Husserl's later work continue to carry with them this suspicion of being investigations of meaning. This is not to say that meanings are purely arbitrary. The phenomenologist is not subjectivist to the extent of investigating only what *he* means. Still, it is difficult to see how "intention" and "meaning" can be adequately distinguished. If every essence is intentional, every essence is *meant*. This can be called "objective," because it is said to be based on "laws" of meaning, but it is no less a *meant* essence. Husserl speaks of the "essence of consciousness," the "essence of perception," the "essence of experience"; but one cannot escape the impression that he is really saying, "the essence of what I *mean*" by consciousness, perception, experience. It is true, of course, that the technique of ideation is supposed to obviate this difficulty, but the suspicion becomes stronger in proportion as the investigations begin to deal with objects about which no initial general agreement can be presumed. In this way the quest for objectivity, which has such an important place in the phenomenological scheme, is slightly tainted with arbitrariness, since it must begin with determining the very essence of objectivity; and Husserl's failure to take history into account makes it possible for him to say what he *means* by objectivity and from then on to

accept as objective what corresponds with this meaning. Perhaps
that is the best anyone can do, but in that case it would seem proper
to recognize the provisional nature of results obtained in this way.

There is no additional problem concerning the objectivity of
the world, since the world is simply described as the sum total of
objectivities present (actually or potentially) to a subject.[1] But
the sum total of objectivity is significant only if we know what
the essence of objectivity is. Once this essence has been determined
on lower levels, it will remain the same on all levels. Now, the
objective as such is described as that which is constituted in constant identity with itself in the operative intentionality of consciousness. In arriving at such an "essential" notion of objectivity
there are two approaches open to the phenomenologist: he can
examine the various meanings which men give, or have given, to
objectivity, and throughout these meanings he can detect an
identical "core" of meaning which he calls its essence; or, he can
submit his own notion of objectivity to all possible variations,
finding in them all an identical element which becomes the essence
of objectivity. In the first case, he is quite obviously arriving at a
least common denominator of meanings, which has the advantage
of representing some sort of common consent, but which is free
from possible error only if common consent constitutes an essence.
In the second case, apart from being, in the concrete, dependent
upon diverse opinions for the content of the variations to which
he subjects the notion, he is limited in his choice of variations not
by some essential "objectivity" which antecedes the variations
themselves, but, since objectivity is an abstraction, by the number
of meanings he is willing to let it have. Husserl, of course, will
have nothing to do with "willing" in this process, since the whole
is controlled by essential "laws" of subjective constitution, but that
simply involves the even greater difficulty of speaking intelligibly
of laws without saying anything of *legislation*. It is all very well
to speak of a terminal "essential intuition," wherein objectivity is
"seen" as it necessarily is; it is still difficult to see how the phenomenologist does more than understand clearly what he constantly

1. Cf. *Ideen I*, pp. 51–52.

means by objectivity — *assuming* that anyone who does not mean the same, *must* be wrong.

It should not be thought that these restrictions invalidate either the phenomenological method or its results. If there is a truly universal subjective a priori, then the meaning at which the phenomenologist arrives at the end of his investigation is not only *his* meaning but the *only* valid meaning that objectivity can have. And, even if this is not true, it has the advantage of making clear to us what Husserl *means* by objectivity, in which case each can decide for himself whether he agrees with Husserl. The phenomenological method, after all, is not one of "proof"; rather, it is one of description, wherein it is *hoped* that others will see things the same way — knowing subjectively that they are wrong if they do not. One can, of course, simply take Husserl's notion of objectivity as a definition — and definitions should not be disputed — examining the whole structure built on this definition to see if it is constantly consistent. This last, of course, is strangely like a mere formal-logical approach, which Husserl decries, but it is difficult to see how he compels us to anything else.

As early as *Ideas,* published in 1913, Husserl asserts that the unique theme of transcendental phenomenology is the subject, within which is contained all objectivity.[2] To this assertion he remains faithful throughout his career; in fact his life work can be considered as an effort to show that a subjective approach to objectivity is not illusory but rather the only approach which can prevent all objective affirmations from being self-contradictory. If the data of consciousness are the only data in no way subject to doubt, then a sure grasp of objectivity must in some way be contained in a grasp of the data of consciousness, or not at all. Thus, to understand individual objectivity is to understand the very constitutive intuition which renders objectivity definitively present to consciousness, and the world, as a totality of objectivity, is to be understood in the same way, by a grasp of the universal constitutive functions whereby it is rendered present to consciousness. Thus, too, just as a comprehension of the constitutive intuition,

2. *Ibid.,* pp. 72–73.

which is intelligible only as constituting objectivity, is by that very fact a comprehension of the object constituted, so a complete grasp of the subjectivity *as constitutive* is a grasp of the world, since only in the constitutive subjectivity is the world to be found as a constant unity of sense.[3] This is the transcendental subjectivity, which is not merely the negative result of a series of "reductions" but is that which positively "precedes the being of the world, in so far as it constitutes within itself the world's sense of being [*Seinssinn* which equals "what it means for the world to be"] and which, consequently, carries entirely in itself the reality of the world as an idea actually and potentially constituted in itself."[4]

Such a subject is not one which *has* experience of the world; it *is* its experience of the world. Subjectivity is, in fact, the complete correlate of the objectivity which is the world; to know it is to know the world, because the world *is* only in its relation to subjectivity. Here we have in a certain sense the finite counterpart of scholastic philosophy's God. Just as the scholastics recognized that a unified world simply cannot make sense except as created by a God who is *subject*; just as Hegel's intuition of world order made him conclude to an original subjective unity which is Absolute Spirit; so Husserl has recognized that a world of sense must have had that sense *given,* and that to say "giver of sense" is to say "subject." Husserl is not thereby necessarily denying God as Creator of the world—although he is singularly indifferent to God in his "philosophic" thought—he is simply asserting that a world of sense *for a subject* must be a world subjectively constituted. The world which I know may be created by God independently of my knowing it, but it is not a world for me until I know it, and it is only in constituting it that I know it. Had Husserl read Saint Augustine he might have concluded that I can constitute a world and thus realize subjectivity only because I am an "image"

---

3. There is something of a tautology here. To understand anything is to grasp its "sense." But, by definition a "sense" is confined to the immanent sphere of consciousness. Therefore, to grasp a "sense" is to grasp what belongs essentially to the immanent sphere of consciousness.

4. *Formale und transzendentale Logik,* p. 237.

of the Creator-God.[5] The fact that he did not so conclude is not proof that he *denied* it, but simply that in cutting himself off from history he could scarcely be complete even as a phenomenologist.

To say that objectivity is constituted in subjectivity, however, is not to say all. This explains its essential relationship to subjectivity; it does not explain its independence of any particular subject. Husserl constantly sought to guarantee the "objective validity" of cognition; and in so doing he was seeking to establish its truth. Now, like Plato in the *Theaetetus,* Husserl was very much concerned that truth be not relative; and he saw, as did Plato, that simply making the subject the measure of objectivity would be relativizing truth.[6] Thus, he goes on to say that subjectivity is the measure of objectivity only when acting in a certain way, a way which will guarantee the elimination of arbitrariness and relativism. Now, if we remember that Husserl insists that subjective operations are subject to necessary laws, we may understand that he can see in a constant identity of constitution at least an indication that these necessary laws are at work. Suppose, for example, that the tree I see when I look out my window is a subjectively constituted tree.[7] If I close my eyes several times and, each time I reopen them, see the same tree; if in addition I leave the house, approach the tree and touch it, go around it and see it from every side; and if the result of all this is the identical unity of sense which I call this tree; then, says Husserl, not only has the tree been constituted in consciousness, but I am sure that it has been constituted in perceptive experience, and hence that the object is truly a tree — it *cannot* be anything else. *Mutatis mutandis* the same sort of subjective constancy in constitution will always be objectively valid:

5. Had Husserl not excluded God from his philosophy he might have hit upon a "self-knowledge" resembling that of Saint Augustine; something which other phenomenologists, such as Max Scheler and Gabriel Marcel, have done.

6. Unlike Plato, Husserl did not recognize that one cannot establish scientifically that there is truth. One can only begin with the supposition that there can be knowledge — and hence truth — after which one can describe the conditions for knowledge (cf. *Theaetetus,* 146A–147A).

7. Tacitly Husserl has accepted the presupposition of Locke, Berkeley, and Hume: that an idea is an *object* of knowledge and not a *means* whereby an object is known.

that is, will always have an object known to be *true*; I can be sure that anyone who sees the object other than as I see it is in error.[8]

Considered in this way subjectivity is something more than a mere correlative of objectivity, in which objectivity is, as it were, mirrored. This would be to make consciousness (*Bewusstsein*) subsequent to being (*Sein*) and thus make *all* consciousness subject to the contingency of existence.[9] Subjectivity is the *a priori source* of objectivity, precisely because experience is a priori, and its apriority is its subjectivity. Subjectivity is the guarantee of objectivity, because only necessity can guarantee truth, and because in the order of cognition only the a priori is necessary. It is not the *fact* of a tree which makes my experience of tree objective; rather it is the apriority of experience which guarantees that such an experience can have a "real" tree and only a tree as its object. Only if we recognize this can we understand a characteristic of Husserl's phenomenology, which Eugen Fink accentuated in his defense of his master, and which has been ignored by so many of Husserl's commentators. In the last analysis, transcendental phenomenology is not so much a *search for absolute being* as it is an attempt to take the world about us and *absolutize it* by constituting it in a consciousness whose necessity is assured, and thus guarantee its objectivity. Based on the principle that the phenomenon is the only source of cognition to which we can appeal, phenomenology understood in this way becomes a systematic effort to transform the naïve acceptance of *a* world into an essential knowledge of *the* world.[10] This result will depend on the extent to which the subject is capable of seeing the world as the objective correlate of an a priori subjective operation. "The world 'has its origin' in us . . . and it is in us that it acquires its habitual influence."[11] This,

8. As a description of the *way* in which we decide that our perceptions are genuinely perceptions and not hallucinations this may well be quite accurate. Whether it is accurate as a description of perception itself is another matter.

9. It is interesting to note that the idealist always sees non-idealism as materialism (e.g. Berkeley), whereas the materialist always sees non-materialism as idealism (e.g. Marx).

10. Eugen Fink, "Die phänomenologische Philosophie Ed. Husserls," pp. 342–43.

11. Cf. *Krisis der europäischen Wissenschaften*, No. 34, pp. 126–35; *Ideen II*, Nos. 50–51.

then, is not a negation of a world-in-itself; it is simply the assertion that such a world cannot have a sense and, hence, cannot *be* in the full sense of the term.[12] Only a world-for-us *is,* and it *is* only to the extent that it has been constituted *in* us.[13]

When we have understood this approach to the world of objectivity we are in a position to understand the phenomenologist's insistence that, although phenomenology is a science of reflection, it is greatly concerned with "pre-reflexive" consciousness.[14] In a certain sense, this aspect of phenomenology has been accentuated more by the followers of Husserl than by Husserl himself, but the latter did not fail to signalize its importance. If consciousness is by definition consciousness-of something, and if reflection is consciousness of consciousness, then prior to any reflection there must be a consciousness of something. Thus, even though phenomenology properly so called begins with reflection, the objectivity with which it is concerned is present in consciousness prior to reflection, and if objectivity is to be understood, pre-reflexive consciousness must be understood as that wherein objectivity first resides. It is not the function of phenomenology to constitute an objectivity different from that which "naïve" consciousness intends; rather, its function is to "clarify" what has already been naïvely intended by constituting and thus guaranteeing it in phenomenological intuition. Nor does this mean that pre-reflexive consciousness is not constitutive; if it is consciousness at all it is constitutive, but only in reflection does it become manifest as such. Thus, when Husserl speaks of a "new constitution" (*Neukonstitution*) or a "reconstitution" of reality he does not mean an operation which is independent of the *original* consciousness in which objectivity is first presented. On the contrary, he means precisely the revelation that the original, pre-reflexive consciousness has been a valid constitution of objec-

12. This Sartre has developed in describing the relationships between the *en-soi* and the *pour-soi.*

13. For a full development of the transcendental subjectivity as the universal a priori, cf. *Formale und transzendentale Logik,* chaps. vi–viii; *Cartesianische Meditationen,* Meditation 3.

14. This point has been much developed by Sartre, Merleau-Ponty, and von Hildebrand, to mention but a few.

tivity. Like Kant, Husserl is convinced that experience is the only immediate contact with reality; but until the constitutive operation which functions in experience has been revealed by reflection, there is no guarantee that the object intended in experience is genuinely valid — no guarantee that what we took to be experience was genuinely experience.

When Husserl transformed the Cartesian *cogito* from an awareness of the substantial being of the *ego*[15] into an intuition of subjectivity as the ultimate a priori source of experience, he recognized the *cogito* as involving a *cogitatum* antecedent to the reflection which validates it. Still, though it is the essence of even naïve consciousness to be a constitution of its own object, it is equally essential to its naïveté not to be aware of its own constitutive operation; and to be unaware of this is to be unaware of its own validity — or invalidity. Once again, then, phenomenology reveals itself as a logic of experience: that is, as an elaborate system for examining experience and discovering the constitutive intentionality which makes it what it is, which reveals it as a priori and hence fundamentally rational, which "judges" it according to the laws of valid intentional constitution and either condemns or acquits it.[16]

It is significant that this examination into experience requires the techniques of epoche and reduction, precisely because thereby pure reflection on experience and hence the revelation of its logic is made possible. As Husserl stated so often, "transcendence" must be bracketed, in order that the contingence and doubtfulness which adhere to it may not impede a truly scientific knowledge.[17] However, it is significant how often he insists that transcendence is to be "bracketed," which is to say, not eliminated. More than that, he insists frequently that transcendence remains, precisely as bracketed. This means that the objectivity he seeks to grasp in an immanent intui-

---

15. Husserl did not make the mistake of interpreting the *cogito, ergo sum* as an inference from thought to existence.

16. Cf. *Krisis der europäischen Wissenschaften*, pp. 143-44, where this is given as the reason why phenomenology is a basis for *all* objective sciences.

17. The very fact that Husserl makes transcendence — or extra-mental reality — the source of contingence and doubt argues that he accepts it as a fact, although not as "being."

tion is the same objectivity which in naïve consciousness is presented as transcendent. If this were not true, phenomenology would reveal itself as a blind search, an attempt to guarantee objectivity without any awareness of the content it is seeking to guarantee. In the second of the *Cartesian Meditations,* Husserl speaks very specifically of the object of naïve experience as a "transcendental guide" in all phenomenological investigation.[18] The notion is not introduced here for the first time, but here it is emphasized as a permanent function of that which has been bracketed in the epoche and reductions. It is nothing more than the content of pre-reflexive consciousness, without which there would be nothing for the phenomenologist to investigate. It is a naïve world, it is true; still it is one which is not destroyed but rather transformed into a consciously constituted and hence guaranteed world. Only thus can we understand Husserl's constant contention that the constitution of the world is not the creation of a world; it is taking a world which is already there and consciously "immanentizing" it in order to remove from it all possibility of doubt.[19]

If we take the objective data with which phenomenological investigation is concerned simply as objective data, they are clearly accessible without all the complicated apparatus which the method invokes. They are *there* prior to the epoche. Still, with the epoche it is as though they were lost, and so it is only an analysis of the constitutive operations oriented toward the objects in question which permits an investigation of the *pure* data of consciousness to rediscover these objects.[20] For phenomenology, an object is simply not susceptible of analysis except to the extent that it is the correlate of an immanent intentional function, so that an analysis of objectivity as such implies a correlative analysis of the intentional function in which it is constituted.[21] The point, however, is that we find

18. *Cartesianische Meditationen,* No. 21; cf. *Formale und transzendentale Logik,* p. 237; also the "noetico-noematic" analyses of *Ideen I.*

19. Cf. *Formale und transzendentale Logik,* No. 71; *Ideen I,* No. 144.

20. The epoche, of course, is never a doubt, not even a methodical doubt. It is simply the eliminating of any position whatever concerning the data of consciousness, so that they can be "reconstituted" without the addition of any element foreign to pure consciousness.

21. The heart of the theory of "noetico-noematic" analysis in *Ideen I.*

here a sort of mutual interaction: objectivity can be properly understood only through the intentional function wherein it is constituted; but the intentional function can be understood only as oriented toward its object — an object apart from the operation which intends it is mere illusion. An intentional operation without the object it intends would be an empty formality.

Now, if there is to be an analysis at all, there must be a point of departure. The key to this point of departure can be found in the essence of the conscious act, which is always consciousness not only of an object but of a determined object.[22] This object has, it is true, been put in parentheses, but as a *determined object* it has been retained as the essential term of the intentional relationship. Precisely, then, because this objectivity furnishes the first element of intelligibility in the intentional structure, it is the object (in parentheses) which is called upon to act as a transcendental guiding thread (*Leitfaden*) for the ensemble of the intentional analysis. There is, for example, no such thing as experience in the abstract; there is only experience of this or that object. If, therefore, one wishes to analyze an experience one must know antecedently *of what* it is an experience. One will find, says Husserl, that the experience has a certain cognitive priority over the object which has been constituted in it, but one cannot *begin* to understand the experience except in terms of the object intended in the experience.

Thus, we can express as a general schema the structure verified in each particular case of consciousness-of in the formula "*ego-cogito-cogitatum*," which is the most general possible schema or "type" of the intentional experience. No matter what the intentional description, it must fit within this framework. If, however, we wish to reduce this to a more particular and hence more concrete form of intentional relationship, it is neither the *ego* nor the *cogito* but the *cogitatum* which reveals its first specification — the formula itself is modified only in regard to the *cogitatum*: from neither the *ego* nor the *cogito* do I get any indication that one experience differs from another. Taking, then, as its point of departure the object immediately present to consciousness, reflection can turn its attention to the actual *mode* of consciousness in which this object is given,

22. Cf. *Cartesianische Meditationen*, p. 78.

as also to the potential modes of consciousness which are contained as a "horizon" in the actual mode, the other "aspects" of the object which are not actually given, but which one recognizes as belonging to the object which is given: e.g., the unseen sides of a cube. In addition, in order that the process of ideation may be complete, reflection looks at the possible modes of consciousness according to which the same object *could* be in consciousness as the identical object of a unified intentional life. In all this the immediate object has not been *changed*; it has been *transformed* and made truly objective.[23]

It is precisely the transformation of this object of pre-reflexive consciousness which brings into strong light the importance of reflection as a phenomenological instrument. If an experience remains only experience, it is, of course, intentional and constitutive, but being naïve it is inadequate to scientific knowledge. In perception, for example, the perceived is the object of a vital experience; it is *given* as this experience, but it is *absolutely* given only to the extent that the experience of perception is itself absolutely given. Thus, to determine that the experience in question is genuinely perception and, hence, that its object is genuinely real, the experience must be made the object of a theoretical examination. Only in this way is the perceived given, as genuinely perceived. Now, clearly, to examine the perception precisely as perception is the work of reflection.[24]

If, then, we examine any act of consciousness whatsoever, there is no question, it will reveal itself as a subjective operation; and as such, says Husserl, it will be a *structure* of subjective components. No act of consciousness, however, is merely that; it is essentially consciousness-of something and thus has an objective side. We might say that the element "consciousness" refers to the subjective act and its subjective components, whereas the element "of something" refers to the object intended in the act. In this second element, Husserl claims, there is a structure corresponding to the subjective structure of the act. Because the objective side is purely *inten-*

23. For this whole analysis of the object as "transcendental guide," cf. *Cartesianische Meditationen*, No. 21.

24. Need we repeat the distinction between reflection and introspection? See *Ideen I*, pp. 145-47.

tional it cannot have any "real" components, but that is not to say that there are no components; they are simply "unreal" or *ideal* components.[25]

Perhaps the most important contribution of the *Ideas* of 1913 was to develop this correlative structure of the intentional act. As he so often did when he wished to emphasize the novelty of a notion, Husserl sought Greek terms to designate the two structures. The subjective (real)[26] structure became the "noetic" structure, or simply noesis; and the objective became the "noematic" structure, or simply noema. There is, unfortunately, a certain confusion in the way Husserl himself employs the term noesis: sometimes designating thereby the intentional act with both its subjective and its objective aspects; sometimes merely the subjective side of the act. In the contrast of noesis and noema, however, it is clear that he does not intend to designate by the two terms two distinct *components* of the vital act of consciousness; rather the terms signify that the one act is structured in two ways, the one real and the other intentional, and can, therefore, be analyzed in two distinct ways. We might say that the noesis is the intentional act *looked at* as a real subjective operation, while the noema is the same act *looked at* as intentionally structured. It is the function of the act as noetic to "give" a sense; it is the function of the same act as noematic to "contain" an objective sense. Now, by reflecting on an act one can discover in it a whole series of subjective modalities which contribute to making it precisely the kind of act it is. It is Husserl's contention that this examination of the subjective modalities of the act reveals the object more and more, because to each subjective modality corresponds an objective modality, and the over-all structure on the objective side corresponds to the over-all structure on the subjective side.[27]

Now, it has always been recognized that the act wherein one ob-

25. *Ideen I*, p. 218; cf. *ibid.*, No. 44, pp. 91–93.

26. It is important to recall the intentional analyses of the *Logische Untersuchungen*, according to which there is never question of "thing-reality" (*Realität*) in the area of consciousness. The word "real" (*reell*) as employed here is opposed to "intentional," not to "ideal."

27. The discussion of noetic and noematic structures forms the central core of the entire section on "Methodology and Problematic of Pure Phenomenology" (*Ideen I*, Part III, chaps. iii & iv, pp. 216–313).

ject is grasped is in some way different from that in which another is grasped; not only is a tree different from a stone, but the perception of a tree is different from the perception of a stone. What Husserl is affirming here, however, is an epistemological principle, according to which it is precisely the difference in the act of perception which reveals the difference in their objects and not vice versa.[28] The difference in acts is such that to every essentially distinct act corresponds an essentially distinct object. Thus, to grasp an act completely is to grasp its object completely, since nothing else could be the object of *this* act. The ideal of philosophy would be to grasp acts so perfectly that their objects would be grasped perfectly. Even where the ideal is not attained, however, Husserl claims that objects can be adequately distinguished in this way. Unfortunately, the examples he ordinarily gives are painfully obvious such as the distinction of tree and stone, or of color and sound, but he intends the principle to be applicable to *all* objects, whether they be events, logical categories, social structures, or abstract qualities, even though the ultimate *nuances* of the objects may not be successfully determined. On this basis the all-important "essential" knowledge becomes a knowledge of how one object is essentially distinct from another. This may not be particularly satisfactory to those who want to know "what things are," but it is doubtful whether "essential knowledge" from Plato to Leibniz was ever any more satisfactory. The advantage is that the distinctions are valid, whether or not anything "exists" corresponding to them. It may be possible that trees and stones cease to exist; it is not possible that tree cease to be distinct from stone — and so for all objects.[29] Incidentally, this theory obviates any discussion as to the "objectivity" of color or any other qualities; if there is a perception of color,

28. There is danger here that the distinction may be merely semantic. Looking at it one way, I know there are different types of *acts* involved, because different *objects* are in question. Looking at it another way, that which makes me aware of different *objects* is the fact of different types of *acts,* since object is an element of act itself.

29. As always, in the "essentialist" position, the influence of mathematics comes to the fore. The non-existing triangle is infallibly distinct from the non-existing square, because it is *logically* impossible to intend the one in place of the other; if I intend triangle I simply do not intend square.

color is objective, since any "existence" outside the perception is irrelevant — green is essentially different from red, whether or not
both red and green are qualities of the perception or of the perceived.

Once more, then, the importance of the object as "transcendental
guide" is brought to the fore. Although the *noematic* structure of
an act is grasped in the grasp of its *noetic* structure, and hence the
object is known in knowing the subjective act which intends it, it
is the naïvely presented object which provides the starting point
for all examination of the act. It is the act which guarantees the
object, but it is the object which specifies the guaranteeing act to
be examined. Without reflection no object is *known*, but without an
object to channel the reflection, the process which terminates in
knowledge cannot even begin. The phenomenologist does not seek
to construct an object out of whole cloth; he wishes to "clarify" the
object he has, in such a way that it becomes *truly* objective. It is
for this reason that the noetic and noematic "structures" are important; only when there is adequate correspondence between the
complex of real and intentional modalities in an act is there a
guarantee that the act is validly objective, which is to say that its object cannot be other than it is.[30]

Nor is this true, according to Husserl, only of perception. Each
general type of consciousness, be it *recall, anticipation, imagination,*
or any conceivable intentional modification, is susceptible of a
similar analysis, terminating in a similar grasp of objectivity on its
own level. Whether or not an object is perceived, recalled, or imagined is to be determined from the character of the intentional
act, not from the existence or non-existence of the object in question.
One imagined object can quite clearly be "essentially" different
from another; and an imagined object can be "essentially" the
same as one which is perceived. Thus, it is important to have two
distinct kinds of analysis, one of which analyzes essentially different *types* of acts, the other of which analyzes essentially distinct

30. Once more, one wonders whether anything more than an analysis of "meanings" is required for this sort of "clarification." Do "essential" distinctions do
anything more than clarify the universe of discourse within which we operate?

95

objects — and both of which complement each other. It is important to note, however, that with the *Ideas,* and thereafter, the accent shifts from the purely noetic analyses of the *Philosophy of Arithmetic* and of the *Logical Investigations* to the noematic analyses wherein the *object* becomes the focal point of the investigation. The study of objectivity gradually becomes a study of the different forms of noemata, the modes of "givenness" which can modify the identical "objective sense," making more manifest its identity and hence its objectivity, without for an instant departing from the data of consciousness alone. The reductions, which at first gave the impression of relinquishing objectivity, have become the guarantee that the ultimate objectivity attained be free from any possible source of doubt or error. Objectivity is determined on a basis of constant identity of sense, but this constant identity of sense is one hundred per cent intentional.

We can exemplify this, as Husserl does in the Second Cartesian Meditation, in the most general way possible by taking the *cogitatum,* divorced from any specific content, as an objective guide. We discover immediately various possible modes of consciousness corresponding to this generality, modes which are differentiated into a series of clearly distinct types — each of them illustrating in its own way the general noetico-noematic structure. Thus, given any object whatever, there are various possible types of intentionality — perception, retention, recall, anticipation, signification — which can be referred to the same object. Then, if this completely general object be given any sort of content, and thus be differentiated, the noetico-noematic structure of the types mentioned is correspondingly differentiated. We can begin, for example, with a logical generality, "something-as-such." [31] This can obviously be broken down into numerous particular objectivities, whether they still be general, such as "the particular," "the universal," "plurality," "totality," "relations," etc., or more specific objectivities, such as logical categories, spatial objects, or animal essences. Each of these objectivities involves an

---

31. *"Etwas überhaupt."* It might, in fact, be better to translate this expression by "merely something." In any case it corresponds to the purely empty "being" with which Hegel begins his *Logic.*

objective type, which acts as a guide in the search for a corresponding intentional structure.[32] Despite the difficulties of analysis, says Husserl, it is clear that the subjective modes connected with such types of objectivity will not be arbitrary; they will, in fact, manifest such a constant identity of structure that the correspondence of objective and subjective structure will always be evident. Thus, an adequate analysis of the subjective structure of the intentional act will reveal all that is to be revealed regarding the object, and there will be no possibility of doubting the result. Just as there is no disputing definitions, there is no disputing the data of consciousness, provided they remain consistent. If one's aim is not to be wrong, there is no better way of assuring that result. If, in addition, one can describe one's "intuition" in such a way that others recognize it as corresponding to their own, one has gone a long way toward communicating the results — phenomenologically.

None of this, of course, is intelligible except in terms of the theory of intentional *constitution* outlined in *Formal and Transcendental Logic*. There the effort has been to get at the ultimate sources of logical concepts, but the result has been a general theory of objectivity as such. Whatever be the *type* of intentionality involved, it is ultimately a type of intentional *constitution* which, when adequately analyzed, reveals the very objectivity of that which it intends. This permits the development of various strict transcendental theories: of spatial objects, of psychophysical essences, of social groups, of cultural objects, and in the last analysis of an objective world as such. No matter what the diversity of theories which can be developed, the ultimate rallying point of all theories will be the most fundamental unity of all, the transcendental *ego*, the center and source of all intentional constitution.[33] Thus, too, every conceivable science is phenomenologically analyzable in such a way as to guarantee its content, but the analysis will be valid only to the extent that it is subsumed

32. Despite the vagueness of all this, we retain Husserl's own examples, in order to avoid an interpretation which would not be Husserl's own.

33. As always, we must return to that which keeps the whole subjective analysis from being arbitrary. The transcendental ego is guided in its constitutive operations by "laws" which assure the objective validity of the results.

under the theory of a universal phenomenology, whose roots are in the transcendental *ego* as such.

From one point of view this can be looked upon as the complete subjectivation of objectivity. According to Husserl, however, it is but the complete validation of objectivity. So long as an intentional theory remains just that — and that phenomenology must remain, at the peril of destroying itself — it is inevitable that an examination of subjective structures, of which objective structures are but correlates, will lead to an examination of subjectivity pure and simple, i.e., to the transcendental *ego*. Therein *all* objects are unified in a universal synthesis, because therein is to be found the proper seat of objectivity — since it is the universal a priori source of objectivity as such. Any object whatever may be chosen as guide in the transcendental investigation; it will necessarily lead to the a priori role which governs its own objectivity and all objectivity, which is to be found in the transcendental *ego*. Every act of consciousness contains a rule for all acts of the same type, and the transcendental *ego* is but the universal unity embracing all types of act. The only hitch in the whole process is that the essence of the transcendental *ego* itself can be determined only as the result of a phenomenological analysis. The ultimate justification of the very source of objectivity, then, can only be that one "sees" it must be this way — a somewhat mystic intuition.

Despite all the confusion involved in presenting objectivity from this new point of view — and it can be understood only in terms of the formal *and* material a priori of which we have already spoken — one thing should stand out clearly: Husserl has no intention of saying that what has always been considered as an object is not an object; he is merely seeking to justify its objectivity without appealing to anything outside consciousness itself. When he says that he grasps the essence of tree or of political society, he is talking about the same tree and the same political society as anyone else. He is simply trying to assure himself that his grasp of it is "scientific," which is to say that he has been able to distinguish it from anything else which may be like it. The suspicion, of course, always remains that he has done nothing more than clarify — for himself and for others

— what he *means* by tree or by political society; in which case he is but seeking what Plato sought long before him — with somewhat less humility than Plato, to be sure, since he does not seem to have recognized the necessity of dialogue in arriving at a *common* meaning.[34]

34. It is here that Gabriel Marcel and Maurice Merleau-Ponty, in particular, have made an advance over Husserl.

6

TRANSCENDENTAL SUBJECTIVITY IN GENESIS

ONE MISTAKE WHICH MUST BE AVOIDED in the approach to the universal a priori source of objectivity, which Husserl calls the transcendental subjectivity, is that of considering it as a sort of ready-made center of conscious activity, which simply produces objective intentions when the occasion demands.[1] In a certain sense, that was precisely the reproach which Husserl leveled against Kant: that the Kantian a priori was simply produced from the subjectivity's own resources, when experience presented it with matter requiring to be informed. As Husserl sees subjectivity, it parallels objectivity so closely that it develops along with the latter. A subject is not by the mere fact of being a subject the a priori source of *all* objectivity. There is no valid objectivity which is not constituted in subjectivity — in this sense it is a universal a priori — but constitution is a continuous flow of conscious operation, wherein one act follows upon another and each prepares for those which are subsequent. Complex objectivities simply cannot be constituted until the subjectivity is rendered gradually capable of the more complicated through the constitution of simpler objectivities. Thus, not only does the objective content of knowledge increase steadily, but subjectivity keeps pace with it, having its own *history* of development as an a priori source. The parallel is such that to follow the development of the one is to follow the development of the other.[2]

It is not likely that any philosopher would dispute Husserl's con-

1. Even where Husserl speaks of the transcendental subject as a Leibnizian "monad," he hastens to assure us that this should not be understood with any "metaphysical" connotations. Cf. *Cartesianische Meditationen*, p. 36.

2. In the Fourth Cartesian Meditation (cf. *Formale und transzendentale Logik*, pp. 183–95) Husserl gives a very good analysis of subjective development or "genesis," paralleling growth in objective experience.

tention that every subject is conditioned in its experiences by the experiences it has already had; that is something of a commonplace. The significance of the contention, however, does not stop there, as can be seen from the very fact that its first consistent development comes in a professedly logical work, the *Formal and Transcendental Logic*. Here there is question, not merely of the subjective conditioning acquired through a series of experiences, but of determining the very truth of judgments in terms of this subjective conditioning. "Transcendental" logic is not concerned merely with the *correctness* of judgments and reasoning processes, but much more with determining when a judgment corresponds with a "state of affairs" and, hence, is *true*. Husserl begins by accepting the Aristotelian characterization of truth as a correspondence between a judgment and the "state of affairs" which the judgment purports to report. Since, however, this correspondence must be determinable entirely within consciousness, there can be no question of using some sort of "independent" reality as a measuring rod of correspondence. The only reality which can have any significance in the investigations is a *constituted* reality, which is but another way of saying that a judgment will be true when the "state of affairs" constituted in it has been phenomenologically guaranteed. All of which brings us back to the a priori *laws* of phenomenological constitution; that is *truly* objective which has been constituted in accord with the *necessary* laws of subjectivity. Thus, the very objectivity of a "state of affairs" reported in judgment is to be determined in a more profound investigation of subjectivity and its "laws."

In order to understand how such a validation of judgment is conceivable, it is necessary to understand the new concept of judgment introduced by Husserl into the discussion. There can be no science unless there is a way of determining when judgments are true; but for the phenomenologist there are two preparatory steps to settling the question of truth: one is to be able to say *what* a judgment is, and the other is to say what a *true* judgment is; and this means grasping the *essence* of judgment and of true judgment. Nor is it a question of beginning with a definition of judgment and remaining consistent with it; rather, it is a question of investigating judgment phenomenologically and discovering what is constantly identical in all its variations.[3] Since a beginning must be made, Husserl takes the Aristotelian S is P as a point of departure,[4] but only as an example which will permit the investigation to get under way.

It might be objected that the Aristotelian predicational form is not a form of judgment at all, but only of the proposition. Its use, however, can be justified, since it is practically inevitable that an analysis of thought will begin with an analysis of language. Language is essentially the incarnation of thought, and to the extent that it is actually calculated to express thought it provides a convenient starting point for analysis.[5] Still, if the analysis is to be more than merely formal it must break away not only from the propositional expression of judgment but also from the prejudice according to which predication is of the very essence of judgment.

Husserl's break with the purely predicative judgment becomes definitive in the *Formal and Transcendental Logic,* but the concept, which in this work comes to the fore, has a history which begins with the inspiration of Franz Brentano, who had so strongly influenced Husserl's early thought. According to Brentano, there is no necessity that a judgment be composed of a subject and a predicate; it consists essentially in a much more elementary act, an affirmation of existence applied to a representation. Thus, the fundamental difference between a single representation and a judgment is the consciousness of existence belonging to the latter, and this is a secondary intentional relation of consciousness to the represented object.[6] Now, this concept is based on a radical realism (involving a somewhat psychologistic interpretation of intentionality), and an equally rad-

3. It may, of course, be doubted whether such an investigation can really take place, unless one begins with at least an implicit definition, which determines the very variations to which the object in question is submitted; but Husserl seems to have been blissfully unaware that such an initial definition could have been determining his whole procedure.

4. Here again we see a hint of an historical procedure, but it ceases being historical as soon as it starts.

5. In both the *Logische Untersuchungen* and *Formale und transzendentale Logik,* Husserl takes language as the starting point for his analyses of thought.

6. Cf. Brentano, *Psychologie vom empirischen Standpunkt,* I, 276–78; *Vom Ursprung der sittlichen Erkenntnis* (Leipzig, 1889; 2nd ed., 1921), p. 15.

ical rejection of the Aristotelian conception of truth as a relation of agreement.[7] Despite Husserl's disagreement with Brentano on the two points mentioned, he came, as a result of his own intentional investigations, to a concept of judgment much broader than that of the Aristotelian ἀπόφανσις. Beginning with the principle that every act of consciousness is consciousness-of something he concludes that every judgment — as an act of consciousness — is judgment-of something and, thus, in itself necessarily ontological.[8] An *immanent* analysis of judgment reveals that it is an intentional act to which is added a "positional" modality. Thus like any other intentional act, it is to be validated by constitutive intentional analysis, not by a comparison of subject and predicate.[9]

The most extended description of the process whereby Husserl arrived at an "essential intuition" of judgment is to be found in *Experience and Judgment,* a posthumous compilation, edited and published by Ludwig Landgrebe. Herein Husserl takes the predicative judgment as an example and finds in it an *essence* which can be verified at various levels, the *highest* of which is the predicative judgment.[10] Thus, when a subject reflects cognitively on an object "given" in a sensible experience, consciousness "retains" the object as a unity of identical elements, which is to say as an object which *is.* Now, though this intentional operation is anterior to the properly predicative moment, it is positional and therefore a judgment. "Every time consciousness gives its attention to something which is and objectifies it, even 'pre-predicatively,' we must call that a judgment."[11] If in a perception an object is given as *being* and is thus *intended,* the perception itself should be considered a judgment, in the broad sense of any "positional" act of consciousness.[12]

7. Heidegger, *Vom Wesen der Wahrheit* (Frankfurt am Main: Klostermann, 1954), pp. 10-12, highlights the fundamental problem of a *relation* between beings of two fundamentally different orders.

8. *Formale und transzendentale Logik,* No. 15.

9. Quite obviously, it is a question of validating the *content,* not the *form,* of this or that determined judgment.

10. Recall the "essential" analysis of evidence, which is apodictic only at its highest level; see *supra,* pp. 75-77.

11. *Erfahrung und Urteil,* p. 62.

12. One wonders whether "judgment" on this level can be anything but tautology.

By thus broadening the conception of judgment, Husserl has made it possible to determine truth on the level of experience, and thus to determine when experience contributes to the development of the subjective a priori and when it does not. That which is genuinely a priori is necessarily valid, and so only an experience which is *true* can be operative in subsequent a priori constitution of valid objectivity.[13] At the same time, because constitution has a process behind it, there is the possibility of tracing that process and thus determining the validity of objectivity in terms of a genesis of constitution itself. Wherever there is authentic knowledge, there is a priori constitution, but neither knowledge (and a fortiori science) nor a priori constitution are possible except in a framework of gradual development. To say that something can be genuinely known is not to say that it can be known by any subject whatever. A child has experiences and is therefore capable of knowledge, but it is capable only of such knowledge as the stream of its previous experiences warrants. When the knowledge comes, its source will be the a priori source of the individual's consciousness, but it will be a source which, precisely as source, has been developed.[14] The same argument applies to the development of consciousness in general — some things can be known only when the knowledge of them has been prepared for historically — but in his published works Husserl did little to develop this insight.[15] In *Formal and Transcendental Logic* and in the *Cartesian Meditations,* however, he does show that he is not entirely unaware that history has a significance. To repeat once more, since his purpose is to develop the method as completely as possible, Husserl, throughout his works, is more concerned with working out the relationship between valid objectivity and transcendental subjectivity than he is with determining the actual results which an intentional analysis of subjectivity can reveal.

13. One is reminded of Marx's limitation of the dialectic of need and fulfillment, whereby he recognizes as valid only that which proceeds from a "legitimate" need.

14. As Merleau-Ponty remarks (*Structure du comportement,* pp. 179–80, n. 1), even modern psychology recognizes that the "innate" need not be present in consciousness from the beginning; it suffices that it be developed from within, drawing on spirit's own resources.

15. Cf. *Krisis der europäischen Wissenschaften.* It is as though Husserl were discovering Hegel's *Phänomenologie des Geistes* for the first time.

If consciousness *becomes* what it is at any stage of its genesis, it should be possible to investigate it genetically, or at least to lay down the rules for such a genesis. Moreover, since it remains true that any intentional investigation must be in terms of both the noetic and the noematic structures of consciousness, an analysis of genetic constitution will reveal both an objective and a subjective side; there will be a "history" of both objectivity and subjectivity. Here, too, objectivity will serve as a transcendental guide for the understanding of subjectivity, which in turn will, when comprehended, throw more light on objectivity. This swinging back and forth between objectivity and subjectivity is not as exceptional as it may seem, especially if, with Husserl, we look on the object with which one begins as a *mere* intention and on subjectivity as the source of verifying intuition, which assures validity *because* it is consciously a constitutive operation. In a certain sense it is illustrated in the ordinary attitude of the scientist. Because he is constantly oriented to knowledge in the strict sense of the term, he is constantly critical of what his judgments *intend*. For that reason he seeks constantly to check them against *objective* evidence. Now, if we say with Husserl that objective evidence is that which has been duly constituted in intuition, we can say that the scientist constantly swings back and forth between mere objectivity and the subjective operation of intuition. In so doing he is gradually increasing his own science and the objective content of what he knows. Without stretching the point too much, then, this might be applied to the whole of conscious life, which will be revealed to have an objective and a subjective development. Learning is not the *accumulation* of scraps of knowledge; it is a *growth,* wherein every act of knowledge develops the subject, thus making it capable of constituting ever more and more complex objectivities — and the objective growth in complexity parallels the subjective growth in capacity.

To speak of a genetic constitution on the objective side is to speak of *essences,* since the full sense of objectivity is contained, not in the concrete individual objects one intends, but only in the objective "sense" of what is intended. This sense, or essence, is necessarily ideal, and it is this which is unchanging in the almost infinite variety of experiences which go to make up a life. Now, no matter what may be said of concrete objects, an ideal sense can come into being only through constitution — and this is true with regard to the sense of judgments as well as of mere representations.[16] Thus, if we take judgment in the broad sense already indicated, we can say that its structure does not appear full-formed, like Minerva springing from the head of Jove, but it must be developed precisely as the unity of objective sense which it is. This is but another way of saying that it has a history, which is to be discovered by returning to the ultimate intentional source of the judgment and tracing it through the noetic and noematic structures whereby it came to be a judgment with this and only this sense. As an ideal unity it is not the term of a *process,* but it can be submitted to a genetic analysis, precisely because the elements of which it is composed have an intentional origin.[17] If one can determine, so to speak, the constitutive series which made this unity of sense possible, one can determine objectively its history. In instituting such an investigation, one is instituting at the same time the constitution wherein the objective sense comes out in its full force.[18] The ultimate scientific judgment will be a predicative judgment, expressed in a scientific proposition, but only if it has been so constituted as the result of a painstaking analysis of the "pre-predicative" elements of which it is constituted will it be, according to Husserl, anything more than haphazard. This is, in truth, no more than a return to the ultimate *evidences* wherein the whole is verified, but, expressed in terms of an historical "tracing-back," it becomes more consciously intentional from beginning to end. There is no science, says Husserl, where there is no apodictic verification of judgments, where there has not been a validation of all the objectivities which enter into every judgment.[19] Finally,

16. Here Husserl's Platonism comes to the fore: the reason why all "being" must be constituted is that only essences are genuinely being, and essences *are* only by constitution. As a matter of fact, it is difficult to assign to "essences" any but a constituted being.

17. Down through history the problem of unity and multiplicity has not been least acute when applied to the ideal unity of the judgment.

18. In *Formale und transzendentale Logik* (e.g., pp. 256–58), Husserl identifies the "true critique of cognition" with intentional constitution (or re-constitution) of naïve objectivity.

19. Cf. *ibid.,* pp. 207–208, 233.

there is no validation of objectivities except in terms of originally constituted evidence, which is to say, in terms of essences which are absolutely known for what they are because they have been constituted in accord with a priori laws.

On the one hand the philosopher may be dismayed at an attitude so thoroughly "scientific." Does Husserl want us to be constantly aware of *all* the evidence involved in all judgments? Is that not condemning philosophy to remain so close to its original intuitions that it will never get beyond them? Although Husserl never puts it this way, neither does he ever deny it. His own constant insistence on a "return to beginnings" condemned his own work to a constant programmatic character; one has the impression that he was never quite satisfied that he was not getting away from the evidence, and thus he is forever beginning all over again. There is no question that there is development in Husserl's thought, but it always seems to be a development in the methodological implications present from the beginning, not an extension of the objective content of philosophical thought, nor even, properly speaking, a genuine explicitation of what was already contained in prescientific thought.[20] Even the extent to which he "rethinks" philosophy as it has presented itself in the course of history is extremely limited; this he leaves to those who will follow him in the phenomenological tradition; they will constitute the "scientific community" within which a strictly scientific philosophy, ever aware of its evidences, is to be realized.[21]

The scientists, on the other hand, look somewhat askance at this science which insists on concerning itself with "essences." Let science concern itself with communicable meanings; yes, but essences, say they, are simply irrelevant. Even those who do not simply reject metaphysics are insistent on keeping it out of science. But Husserl persisted in his claims that science itself is not adequately

20. E.g., *Ideen II* and *III,* which are concerned with constituting the framework within which a phenomenological psychology and philosophy of nature can be carried out, while saying very little with regard to the "content" of these disciplines.

21. It would seem that in later years Husserl had lost the hope that this "scientific community" would ever assemble.

scientific, so long as it does not grasp the essences involved in the very concepts with which it is concerned. Not only must the scientist be able to say what he means by the concepts he uses; the concepts must be so objectively determinable that no one who thinks rightly can use them in any other way.[22] The appeal to intuition, however, is an appeal to a kind of evidence which simply has no meaning for the scientist as scientist — precisely because it is an appeal to universal a priori laws of subjectivity which are not scientifically "verifiable."

It is perhaps in answer to this last criticism that Husserl attempts in the Fourth Cartesian Meditation to describe the concrete genesis [23] of the universal *a priori,* which is the transcendental subjectivity, concretized in the *person.* Up to the present the synthetic unity of all evidences has been described as an ideal; whether or not it can be realized depends on whether there really is an evidence which embraces all. If objectivity is essentially — or by definition — that which is constituted in subjectivity, then there can be no objectivity which is not so constituted. Still, in order that subjectivity be the "evidence" of objectivity it must be known as thus constitutive. How is it known? Husserl's answer is that subjectivity is constituted concomitantly with objectivity; as constituted it is not abstract but concrete.

Such a constitution, however, cannot be the same as objective constitution; if it were it would simply be an objectivation of subjectivity, which has its place, but which contributes nothing to the question at issue. The transcendental subjectivity must be grasped as it is, which is to say, it must be constituted; but it must remain as it is, which is to say, as the essentially non-object. To illustrate the difficulty of grasping the transcendental subject as a concrete unity of consciousness we can take an individual subject at three moments of its continuous conscious life: at birth — in the sense of a "com-

22. As has already been pointed out, it is the "essential intuition" which makes the difference between a mere analysis of meanings and a universal phenomenology of reason (see *supra,* Chap. 5, pp. 95, 97, nn. 30, 33).

23. The description, of course, is wholly in the abstract, but it purports to explain what must be the development of *any* concrete subjectivity.

mencement" of experiences; after the acquisition of a variegated multiplicity of experiences; and lastly, after the acquisition of science, in which these experiences are verified and systematized. In one sense the subject is always the same; in another sense it is never the same. As transcendental, the subject is inseparable from its experiences, which is to say, it is inseparable not only from its acts but also from the objective correlates of these acts. Thus, as we have already said, objects are objects only *for* the subject; they are constituted objects by being related to a subject. Conversely, the subject is subject because it has objects; it is constituted subject by its relation to objects. This means that a subject, precisely as subject, can be present to consciousness only in virtue of the object it intends.[24] A subject thus understood is determined (and constituted) as subject precisely in constituting objects. Now, the sum total of objects, to which corresponds the sum total of relations to objectivity which is the subject, is constituted as a succession of objects governed by an *order* operative in their constitution. On the subjective side, then, there is a corresponding order in constitution, not an order of successive *isolated* intentional acts, but an order of constantly "flowing" consciousness.[25] Thus, the three moments of conscious life mentioned above are separable from the stream only by abstraction; it is in the continuous flow of objectively constitutive operation that the subject is constituted as subject. It is throughout the *same* subject as an identical center of reference for its objective correlates; it is a constantly different subject as constantly *growing* with its own experiences. Objective constitution, then, is the "life" of the subject, and it is constituted as subject *in* and *through* this "life."

The subject thus constituted is neither the mere objectivation of intentional relationships, to which a unity has been given by thought, nor a substantial subject, *à la* Descartes, which, according

24. If, *per impossibile,* there were absolutely no difference in the objective correlates of two subjects, they would not be two but one.

25. A subject to which Husserl devoted *Phänomenologie des inneren Zeitbewusstseins* and a whole series of late manuscripts, preserved at Louvain and grouped under the catalogue letter C.

to Husserl, is an unjustified inference *from* the data and not at all contained *in* the data.[26] What is contained in the data, he says, is an *ego* identified with the flowing life of experiences and at the same time an *ego* which lives and *has* the experiences in question. This is what subjective constitution means: the identity of subject as constant source of objectivity.

It is here that Husserl treats subject in a way for which we have not been prepared. It is not, he says, a mere empty center of reference for objectivity; it is the substrate, though not substance,[27] of a vital series of habits (*Habitualitäten*), a substrate which, by the law of transcendental genesis, gains with each act proceeding from it a new and durable characteristic, which conditions the subsequent acts proceeding from it. Thus, its unity is more than the unity of actual continuity of experience, which would be broken by sleep; it is the continuity of a living subjectivity, where potentiality plays as important a part as actuality — potentiality understood not as mere passive capacity but as a positive conditioning by previous acts. Thus, every act of consciousness passes, but it leaves behind the *ego* which performed the act, and which by virtue of that act is rendered capable of a subsequent act of which it was not really capable before. The child has a *passive* capacity for becoming a scientist, but it is rendered really capable of science only by the actual experiences, gained over a period of time, which, by leaving an habitual residue, condition the very subjective a priori which is to be the source of truly scientific judgments.

This continued subjective identity is the personal character which permits the subject to say "I," to be not merely an abstract subjectivity but a concrete subject. Only within a subject thus understood can we comprehend another form of development which Husserl introduces in the Fourth Cartesian Meditation. There is in the subject, he says, not only the active genesis of conscious activity,

26. Cf. *Formale und transzendentale Logik*, p. 204; *Krisis der europäischen Wissenschaften*, pp. 76–83.

27. The term "substance" always bothered Husserl, since for him it implied the sort of physical causality which belongs to material things. His own notion of "substrate," however, is not too different from the scholastic "substance."

but also the passive genesis of *association*. In investigating consciousness it is impossible to begin with any but a consciousness which already manifests a certain development — there is no hope of arriving at any *first* act of consciousness. Thus, the first indication we have of any "process" in the constitution of objectivity is when the *ego* consciously constitutes the essence of that which was heretofore naïvely present to it. This sort of constitution we can qualify as "active," not in the sense of a return to psychological activity, but in the sense that it is an operation of what Husserl calls (in the broad sense) the "practical reason," which is to say, an operation wherein the subject, by reworking a fund of pre-given objects, constitutes objectivities which are new in relation to the pre-given objects, precisely because they have their origin in an operation which is distinct from that of simply grasping objects as presented. Thus, various synthetic forms enter consciousness, because they have been constituted in synthetizing acts of consciousness. This is the sort of constitution of which the mathematician and the logician are keenly aware.[28]

Now, it seems clear enough that such forms are not part of the concrete *ego* simply as such; in childhood, for example, they are not actively present.[29] Still, it can be said that, even prior to the **actual synthesis operated by consciousness, the "materials" with which reason works are present to consciousness.** These "materials" are *pre-given* with respect to the spiritual activity of constitution implied in their synthesis,[30] but they are not pre-given in the sense that they are independent of constitution; nothing is.[31] Rather, in relation to the synthesis they *have been* constituted, not actively but "passively," because they belong, as it were, to the constant spontaneous operation of consciousness. This matter (of synthesis) is not simply there, as though received from without; it is constituted in an intentional operation of consciousness, which is to say that

28. As early as the *Logische Untersuchungen,* Husserl was vaguely aware of this in his pages on "categorial intuition"; cf. Investigation VI, chap. vi.

29. Kant never sought to explain the origin of the a priori forms of reason.

30. Cf. *Cartesianische Meditationen,* p. 112; *Formale und transzendentale Logik,* p. 195.

31. Cf. *Formale und transzendentale Logik,* p. 208.

some time in the past its constitution was *active*.[32] Thus, even in infancy there is no merely *given* experience of "thing"; the child must learn to experience objects as "things," and this is to constitute the objectivity "thing." Further progress in experience, then, consists in the further specification of "things" thus constitutively given. In relation to these further specifications the given objectivity, "thing," can be looked upon as *passively* constituted. Thus, "passive constitution" is never more than *relatively* passive, relatively to further intentional operation.

Still, it is not sufficient to recognize the presence of these "materials" of synthesis; Husserl demands an essential intuition of a veritable process of passive constitution, which consists precisely in the constant presence of objectivities which are "associated" prior to any active effort at synthesis. What is more, given an active synthesis of materials, the result persists and functions passively in subsequent active synthesis. This passive persistence of active synthesis effectuated in the *ego* forms the habits, which determine the conscious activity of the subject at this or that point of time in its development.[33] Thus, one can speak not only of a passive constitution of objectivity but also of subjectivity; the a priori which is subjectivity grows in proportion to the *horizon* of objects which increase the subject's range of further actively constitutive intentional operations.[34]

Passive genesis (both of objectivity and of subjectivity) is, then, only relative, which is to say, relative to the act wherein an object is grasped as pre-given, as material for an active synthesis. Such an object, precisely as object, *had* an active genesis, *was* actively constituted. However, by virtue of the fundamental principle of passive genesis, which is *association,* the synthesis is "motivated"[35] and, hence, never simply arbitrary. By a sort of *tour de force* Husserl

---

32. A point which causes Husserl no little trouble, since no amount of effort can bring him back to the beginning of constitution. Cf. *Cartesianische Meditationen,* pp. 112–13.

33. The merest hint of a "dialectic of consciousness," which is not developed dialectically.

34. Cf. *Cartesianische Meditationen,* pp. 114–21.

35. Cf. *Ideen II,* Part III, chap. ii, Nos. 54–61.

has reintroduced the concept of *causality* into cognition; not a *physical* but a *spiritual* causality, i.e. a relation of ideal, unreal intentions. Nor is this an "association of ideas" *à la* Hume, since it quite clearly repudiates any "naturalistic" explanation of the passive synthesis.[36]

Though it is difficult to see how the "laws" of such passive synthesis can be determined, Husserl insists that a combination of the essential laws of intentional constitution as such and those of temporality — both of which are grasped in intuition — prescribes an essential *order* in constitution. This essential order makes it possible to understand and interpret the elements of the "passive synthesis," both on the objective and the subjective level. It is unfortunate that Husserl remained so constantly vague on this point, but perhaps a certain vagueness is the price one pays for avoiding a conception of association according to the empirical laws governing the life of the spirit.[37] Husserl's aim, after all, is not to explain the genesis of some individual objectivity, but rather to lay down the principles governing the intentional constitution of the transcendental *ego* as source of all objectivity as such. Such a concrete[38] transcendental subject is liable to a complete misunderstanding if it is not interpreted in terms of a temporal sequence of development. Only in terms of temporality can intentional constitution escape the danger of being interpreted as an arbitrary mental projection. It is essential for a comprehension of the *ego* to understand that each stage in its genetic process is an intentional operation subject to laws governing the whole process. In the (concrete) developed *ego* the structure of development by temporal stages is a systematic form of associative perception governing objective constitution — which in turn conditions its subjective counterpart.

Right there we run into one of those difficulties which are constantly manifesting themselves in transcendental phenomenology

36. Cf. *Formale und transzendentale Logik*, pp. 226–27; *Philosophie als strenge Wissenschaft*, p. 317; *Nachwort zu meinen Ideen*, p. 16.

37. Can the phenomenologist ever really communicate with the non-phenomenologist? What meaning can a description of experience have for one who does not experience in the same way as does the one describing? Cf. *Nachwort zu meinen Ideen*, p. 2.

38. Husserl is convinced that "essences" are concrete.

and which threaten to make its investigations interminable. Each time that a concept is introduced into an explanation, it is necessary to submit the concept itself to an intentional analysis, so that it may be grasped scientifically and thus fit into the scientific character of the whole — otherwise a non-scientific element would endanger the whole structure.[39] Husserl had, it is true, investigated the concept of temporality long before the *Cartesian Meditations,* but since he had in the meantime devoted a whole series of unpublished manuscripts to renewed discussions of the same troublesome notion, one has the impression that he himself was not too satisfied with his own attempts to understand it scientifically. In the *Formal and Transcendental Logic* and the *Cartesian Meditations* it is as though temporality no longer presented any serious problems and could be taken for granted; in fact, however, it presents to scholars one of the outstanding difficulties in attempting to interpret Husserl's thought. The one published study which he devoted to the investigation of time, the *Phenomenology of the Inner Consciousness of Time,* though edited by Martin Heidegger in 1927, was actually written by Husserl prior to *Philosophy as Rigorous Science* and *Ideas I.* Thus, it represents an early and somewhat undeveloped stage in Husserl's thought. What is more, it is concerned with a problem quite distinct from (though related to) that which arises in discussing the temporality of intentional constitution itself. As the title indicates, it is concerned with investigating the consciousness which has temporality for its object; while in *Ideas I* as in *Philosophy as Rigorous Science,* the accent is put on the temporality of consciousness, in so far as it is essential to every act of consciousness that it be temporal.[40] Taken in this sense, not only does every intentional act have a temporal extension, but temporality is also a necessary form uniting act with act.[41] Thus, the temporally extended intentional act fits into a temporal continuity of acts. It is temporality looked at in this way which is important for an understanding of genetic constitution, whether objective or subjective.[42]

39. It would seem that a perfectly consistent phenomenology would involve a thorough-going and constant linguistic analysis.
40. *Ideen I,* p. 196.
41. Cf. *ibid.,* pp. 198, 291–93.
42. *Cartesianische Meditationen,* pp. 109–11.

As was mentioned before, the *essences* with which phenomenology is concerned differ from mathematical concepts precisely in their refusal to be grasped with the same "exactitude" with which the objects of mathematical science can be grasped. Mathematical essences can be *fixed* in such a way that they are completely independent of temporality — their eternity is an eternity of fixity. The concept of "mathematical triangle," for example, is in no way affected by the temporal sequence of experiences which precede it, nor is it in any way modified by subsequent experiences.[43] The "ontological" essences of phenomenological science, on the other hand, can never be independent of temporality; they are understandable only as temporalized. This does not mean, according to Husserl, that the grasp of them is any less scientific than the grasp of mathematical essences, but it is a grasp which is scientific only because it takes temporality into account. The very transcendental subject, which is the a priori source and center of all scientific knowledge, is itself temporalized. The time which is here in question has little in common with "cosmic" time, which can be measured; still it has two characteristics which justify its being designated by the same term: it involves a continuous *succession,* and this is an *ordered* succession.

In analyzing the essence of objective time, Husserl has discovered in it the order of the before and the after, which we might call its "irreversibility." What is before necessarily precedes that which is after, and this constitutes a certain dependence of the after on the before. This by no means necessarily implies a relation of *causal* dependence,[44] but it does mean that the after cannot be if the before was not. Now, obviously the last statement *could* be a mere tautology, but Husserl clearly does not intend it as such. The "laws" of temporality determine not only a general sequence of before and after but also *what* comes before and *what* after. This can be applied first of all to an individual act of consciousness, perception for example. Since the act of perception cannot be fixed in any instant, it necessarily involves in its very being a retention or "has perceived"

43. The complete accuracy of this might well be disputed, but that temporality would at least play an entirely different rôle in mathematical concepts seems indisputable.

44. Husserl agrees with Hume in rejecting any knowledge of causality in this sense.

and an anticipation or "will perceive." There is an essential order of the before and after, even in this simplest of examples. But the individual act is possible only as an "abstraction," whereby it is mentally isolated from the continuous stream of perceptions — and if it were to be taken only in this isolated form it would be a falsification of its essence as perception, which is possible only in a larger temporal continuity. Ultimately the overall temporal continuity or "stream" will be history; but it is precisely here that Husserl's analysis falls down: he assures us that consciousness, in its noetic and noematic structures, is historical, but he gives us no means of determining the significance of this history. We misunderstand consciousness, he tells us, if we see it other than as temporal, or if our "seeing" is other than temporal, but he gives us no clear indication of what this temporalization makes of objectivity or of subjectivity. One gets the impression that Husserl analyzes essences *as though* they were atemporal and then warns us that they *are* temporally modified and can be understood properly only "if this temporality is taken into consideration." [45]

When, however, in the Fourth Cartesian Meditation, Husserl speaks of the genesis of subjectivity, we do begin to see some significance in temporality, particularly from the point of view of succession and order in development. The *possibility* of all objectivity is contained in the a priori of subjectivity; but possibility does not mean *compossibility*. There is a strict order of before and after in possibility. There is no objectivity which is not constituted in subjectivity, but there is an essential order in this constitution, so that the very essence of what is constituted *after* is conditioned by what has been constituted before. Further, the subject, which is somewhat paradoxically always the same and yet never the same, is the a priori source of objectivity only to the extent that it follows a rigid order of development. The mutual interdependence of objectivity and

---

45. In reference to *Philosophie als strenge Wissenschaft*, p. 316, cf. Dilthey's remark: "A true Plato, who first of all fixes in concept the things that become and flow, then puts beside the concept of the fixed a concept of flowing." *Gesammelte Schriften*, Vol. V, p. cxii; it is cited by Georg Misch, *Lebensphilosophie und Phänomenologie* (Leipzig: Teubner, 1931), p. 136.

subjectivity follows an essential order, which, because it is essential is discoverable. It is precisely the discovery of this order, however, which is the unsolved problem — the problem of history. Phenomenologically speaking, "discovery" is "constitution," and thus the very order of constitution must be constituted. Nor is it clear how one can break out of the circle in a theory which, consciously at least, admits of no dialectic. We shall see later that the theory of "intersubjective constitution" is an attempt to break out of the circle, but one wonders if any attempt can be successful, so long as constitution remains only constitution, so long as "to be given" is unequivocally identified with "to be constituted."

Be that as it may, the theory of temporality, vague as it remains, does help to elucidate the constitutive a priori of phenomenology in terms of learning. According to Husserl, not only is there an ordered succession observable in the process of learning — again on both the objective and subjective side — but at least the general structure of this temporal succession is susceptible of an essential intuition. Lest it should seem, however, that this would involve the possibility of complete prediction in the learning process, we must understand this as a concrete intuition of a specific temporal synthesis. Unfortunately, such an affirmation is hopelessly vague; it tells us little more than that an ordered succession in learning is inevitable and that it is possible to go back in reflection and retrace the genesis of the concrete personal subject. This retracing is a *constitution,* by which is meant that a vague recognition of process is transformed into an exact knowledge of a specific course in development, in terms of which any individual act of knowledge or any individual objectivity in the series must be interpreted. In this sense, the theory of temporality can be looked on as an elucidation of the contention that all objectivity is known in an adequate knowledge of subjectivity. And yet, this is hardly an elucidation with regard to *what* is known, only with regard to the *way* it is known.

7

A UNIVERSAL PHENOMENOLOGY OF REASON

DURING HIS PHILOSOPHICAL CAREER Husserl faced the inevitability of modifying his original project in many ways. If we look at the *Philosophy of Arithmetic* or even at the first edition of the *Logical Investigations,* we uncover a notion of "eternal truth" which tries to resemble the kind of results which can be achieved in mathematics. As time went on, however, Husserl realized more and more clearly that this was not the sort of thing one could expect in philosophy, whose essences simply could not be fixed mathematically. As vague as his concept of "reality" may have been, he was aware that philosophy had to be concerned with reality in some sense of the term, whereas mathematics was justified in prescinding entirely from any question of reality. Because this was true, philosophy had to be rooted in experience, which, no matter how analyzed, is the subject's first and only direct contact with reality. What is more, since experience is essentially temporal, the essences which involve experience must be considered in terms of the modifications which temporality introduces, if they are not to be misunderstood. We shall see later that other modifications must be introduced, if subjectivity is to break the bonds of individuality and be truly universal in any but an abstract fashion.

Despite successive modifications, however, there are two elements of Husserl's original theory which do not change down to the very end. If philosophy is to be philosophy at all, he continues to insist, it must be strictly scientific, which is to say, it must provide a knowledge which is in no sense merely opinion or "belief," a knowledge which does not come about accidentally but is the result of consciously applied methods.[1] Likewise, there is no point in speaking

1. In *Philosophie als strenge Wissenschaft* (p. 341), Husserl claims that geniuses

of philosophy, if it is not to be a science of *essences*. Positive science can tell us *how* things do and will *act,* but only philosophy can tell us *what* things *are.* A science which does not tell us that is simply not philosophy. The modifications which have been introduced are a recognition that one cannot have too much naïve confidence that one's investigations have terminated in a knowledge of essence as it really is, but they are also an attempt to save the science of essences. Too many objections could be raised against the sort of intentional analyses practiced in the *Logical Investigations* or even in *Ideas I,* but Husserl's answer to the objections is not to abandon the ideal of science through intentional analyses. Rather it is to refine the intentional analyses in such a way as to account for "real" differences of essences *within* the framework of the immanent intentionality of consciousness.

Thus, we see that Husserl refuses to abandon the attempt to synthesize Descartes' ideal of a universal science — *mathesis universalis* — with Kantian transcendental idealism. He will not accept the dualistic prejudice of Descartes, which insists on working from the existence of consciousness. Nor will he accept Kant's limitation of science, according to which a being is recognized which can be *thought of* but which cannot be scientifically *known.* Husserl's ideal is a universal science, and he will retain the ideal, even if the price he has to pay is the complete subjectivizing of all objectivity and the simple identification of being with what *can* be scientifically known. The synthesis of the two ideals requires that he admit nothing which cannot be an object of science and that he accept no other source for the necessity which belongs to the scientific knowledge than consciousness itself. With Kant, however, he will designate the subjective "faculty" in which necessity resides by the name "reason." Thus, the only ultimate source of science in the strict sense must be reason; and if phenomenology is to be an investigation of consciousness, then the phenomenology which is to be a universal science must be an investigation of reason, in the sense that it determines how and when reason is operative.

of the past have attained to truth by unconsciously applying the method of eidetic analysis. Cf. *Krisis der europäischen Wissenschaften,* pp. 16–68, on Galileo.

For Husserl as for Kant, though the term "faculty" (*Vermögen*) may be applied to reason, it is not to be considered as some sort of entity in any way distinct from consciousness. Reason is consciousness acting in a special way. For Kant it is consciousness acting in accord with a priori rules which ensure the validity of its objects, because they contribute to the act of consciousness precisely the necessity which makes it knowledge. For Husserl it is constitutive consciousness, wherein are constituted not only objectivities but, what is more important, objectivities which cannot possibly be other than as constituted. The critique of such a reason does not demand a criterion whereby its objects can be evaluated; it is its own guarantee by the very fact that it is reason.[2] Husserl is perfectly consistent in demanding that all knowledge and science have none but an immanent validation, and so the criterion of validity becomes the fact of constitution in reason. This is dangerously close to the sort of psychological necessity of thinking which Husserl definitively repudiated in the first volume of the *Logical Investigations* and in *Philosophy as Rigorous Science*, but he persists in claiming that here is an entirely different kind of necessity. This sort of necessity is extremely important, for it permits Husserl to achieve the goal he had constantly before him, the complete rationalization of experience.

By the very logic of his own original principles, Husserl has been pushed to the most radical rationalism of which human thought would seem to be capable. Since the beginning of recorded thought philosophers have struggled with the problem of reconciling reason and experience, and down through the ages the solutions have ranged from the completely irrational surrender to experience, which hardly merits the name of philosophy at all, to the complete domination of experience by reason, which is but another way of expressing pure idealism.[3] Between the two extremes there have been a large variety of positions, which can be characterized by

2. A "critique" of reason simply has the function of assuring one that it *is* reason which is operative in cognition.

3. The complete surrender to experience is commonly connected with the name of Heraclitus; whereas the exclusive stress on reason is credited to Parmenides. Modern scholars are less hasty in interpreting two of philosophy's "greats."

their proximity to either of the two extremes. What has always been characteristic of the intermediate positions is that they have retained the distinction between reason and experience, now stressing the role of experience with Heraclitus or Nietzsche, now concentrating on reason with Parmenides or Kant, or attempting a perfect synthesis of the two with Hegel and the German idealists. The extremes have seldom been touched, since they have always seemed to require an utter disregard of either reason or experience.

In this sense Husserl's effort is genuinely new. With the *Logical Investigations* he announced that philosophy "will be a completely rational science," [4] but it will do so without in the least disregarding experience. Nor will it attempt an Hegelian synthesis of reason and experience, which requires submitting to a dialectic law over which human reason simply as human reason has no control, a law which is, so to speak, above both reason and experience. Husserl *wants* to regulate the relationship of reason and experience according to a law which is intrinsic to both.[5] This does not involve disregarding either; instead, it involves suppressing the distinction between the two. In tune with the history of philosophy, Husserl will, on the one hand, credit experience with an *immediate* contact with reality, but he will seek to suppress the contingency commonly assumed to be involved in immediacy. On the other hand, he will credit reason with necessity in its grasp of reality, but he will accept no mediation in reason's operation.[6] The result, then, is a necessary experience and an immediate reason — which is but another way of saying a "rational experience" and an "experimental reason." [7]

The possibility of this identification did not come to Husserl all at once. It began when he discovered the effectiveness of a theory of intentionality in explaining the genesis of logical categories. It grew

4. *Logische Untersuchungen*, I, p. 207; cf. *ibid.*, p. 231.
5. In *Philosophie als strenge Wissenschaft* (p. 292), Husserl stresses the voluntary aspect of this insistence that there be a *rational* solution.
6. This is, perhaps, the fundamental point of disagreement with Hegel, who insists on the role of "mediation" in all "scientific" knowledge. Cf. Henri Niel, *De la médiation dans la philosophie de Hegel* (Paris: Aubier, 1945).
7. *Formale und transzendentale Logik*, No. 94; cf. *Cartesianische Meditationen*, pp. 91–97; *Ideen I*, Nos. 144, 149.

with the further realization that an intentional explanation of *all* essences would eliminate all contingency by making the *content* of consciousness as assured as the *act* of consciousness itself. Since, however, he was convinced that the content of consciousness could be effectively guaranteed only by *intuition,* the logic of immanent analysis forced him to make of intuition an *intentional* function. The reconciliation was long in coming, but consistency made it inevitable that an intentional intuition be looked on as a *constitution* of essences. There evolved with a theory of constitution the possibility of a non-mediated grasp of philosophy's ultimate object, i.e., of essences. Now, if there is a grasp of essences at all, it must be through reason, since by definition essences are necessary objects, and, again by definition, reason is the faculty of necessary objects.[8] Thus, with the theory of constitution Husserl had hit on the possibility of an immediate rational grasp of reality, which is but another way of saying a completely rationalized experience.

Quite obviously Husserl's problems were not at an end with the "discovery" of rationally constitutive experience. It was still necessary to account for the temporal flow of consciousness in grasping essences, to say nothing of the non-fixity of the essences grasped, where "to grasp" is "to constitute." It was still necessary to explain the possibility of error in a consciousness from which every source of error would seem to have been eliminated. Finally, it was necessary to break out of the solipsistic circle which subjective constitution would seem to imply. It is significant, however, that the problems which persist never raise any doubts in Husserl's mind as to the validity of constitutive intentionality.[9] He may not *have* the solution, but he is convinced that the solution is to be found in the theory.[10] Never once do we see him considering even the possibility

8. One is again reminded of Plato's illustration of the "divided line," where to every determinate characteristic in objects must correspond a determinate characteristic in the subjective grasp of the object.

9. Not even the most sanguine phenomenologist would pretend that these problems have been "solved." The solutions which have been offered involve a certain unfaithfulness to purely constitutive phenomenology; e.g. those offered by Scheler, Heidegger, Merleau-Ponty, Sartre, and von Hildebrand.

10. Husserl is slightly less than phenomenological in all this. He had simply *de-*

of an alternative. Strictly speaking, the theory is never "modified"; it simply recognizes progressively that more elements must be clarified.[11]

In the manuscript of *Ideas III,* which Husserl himself left unpublished, he introduced the notion of constitution as a "clarification" of intentions. In the framework of the "reductions" already described, this means completely "immanentizing" already present intentions in order to give the sort of validation which phenomenology demands throughout. If it meant only this, however, it would hardly represent an advance over the thought of *Ideas I* and would not merit being taken up again and stressed in *Formal and Transcendental Logic.* But, if we compare the notion of "validation" in phenomenology with that of "verification" in positive science, we may see how "clarification" contributes to a better understanding of ultimate constitution. To verify phenomenologically is to guarantee the necessary objectivity of the essence intended — i.e., by intuition. To verify scientifically is to check a proposition with experience, the only condition under which the proposition can be said to be "meaningful." To clarify is both to validate and to verify — involving the necessary objectivity of what is intended by reason and the meaningfulness of what is the object of experience. Thus, clarification means the reconstruction in reason of that which has already been constituted simply as an object of consciousness. It is "original" constitution, in the sense of a return to the only possible original contact with reality, i.e., to experience. It is "rational" constitution, in the sense of imposing a necessity on thought — not merely the necessity of thinking in a certain way, but the necessity that thinking in this way be correct and therefore true.[12]

cided early in his career that the skeptical position of Hume is unacceptable. This means that there *is* a solution. Since, however, he had followed Hume to the extent of burning all bridges behind him, the solution had to be found by going forward along the only path still open.

11. Those who most vigorously decry "dogmatism" frequently find it difficult to avoid being dogmatic. Cf. Friedrich Engels, *Anti-Dühring* (Berlin: Dietz, 1953), p. 99; *Dialektik der Natur* (Berlin: Dietz, 1952), pp. 19, 28.

12. This necessity, of course, depends on a conformity with "transcendental laws" of thought, which themselves must be *intuited.*

What Husserl is equivalently attempting with this "new" theory is not so much to establish the validity of any particular objectivities as to establish once more a theory of cognition which will provide a guarantee for any objectivity simply as such. In *Ideas II* and *Ideas III* this is done on a modified scale by seeking to provide an adequate basis for scientific knowledge of "spirit" (psychology) and of "nature" (philosophy of nature). The project of *Formal and Transcendental Logic,* however, is far more ambitious. It will do for logic itself what logic had attempted to do for the particular sciences. In this, according to Husserl, he was restoring the Platonic ideal of science:[13] to give logic a true and adequate foundation, to validate the very science which validates other sciences, thus establishing a new universality of science. This new science would take absolutely nothing for granted, not even logic itself;[14] it would be a theory to establish a basis for the authentic essence of knowledge itself. Here, then, it is not a question of developing a higher-level theory of cognition; rather, it is a question of laying the foundations which will make a theory of cognition a real possibility at all.

Thus, *Formal and Transcendental Logic* does not question merely the validity of some particular science, or even of all sciences, to validate them by applying to them norms taken from outside the sciences themselves. It will question the very possibility of science as such, a question which can be answered only by determining the very essence of science.[15] If this can be determined, then a universal theory can be set up, with which science will have to conform, if it is to be rational knowledge at all. Now, this is not entirely new in Husserl's thought,[16] but here it is approached from a new angle. It is still a question of validating the basic concepts of any science — a task which the particular science cannot even pretend to accomplish — but it is to validate by determining the laws according to which any concept whatsoever can and must be validated. Husserl will

13. *Formale und transzendentale Logik,* p. 1.

14. Husserl had accused Kant of naïvely assuming the validity of formal logic; he would question even this, *ibid.,* p. 229.

15. By an "eidetic intuition" of *what* science is.

16. It is present in the *Prolegomena zur reinen Logik* and in *Philosophie als strenge Wissenschaft.*

establish a universal criterion of validity; any concept which does not conform to it simply cannot lay claim to validity. The result may find no difference whatever in the contents of the sciences, but it will mean all the difference in the world in the *way* these contents are known. It is for this reason that the result is to be called a "universal" theory of science; no element of any science can escape its normative function.

As far back as the *Philosophy as Rigorous Science*, Husserl had insisted that up to his time philosophy had simply not existed, because up to his time it had simply not been scientific.[17] Now that statement takes on added meaning, since no matter how scientific a philosophy may claim to be, if it fails to provide a sure basis for any element of any science, it is to that extent itself "naïve" and therefore not a strict science. The difficulty here, of course, is that, since phenomenology itself has not effectively proved its applicability to all sciences, it, too, cannot lay claim to the title of strict science. To this objection there are in reality three answers in Husserl's thought: (1) phenomenology is a strict science in the sense that it contains within itself the only possibility of even aiming at such an ideal. Incidentally, this makes phenomenology also applicable to future advances in science without so systematizing knowledge that everything must simply by definition fit in.[18] (2) If it is claimed that there is anything to which phenomenology does not apply, that can simply be left out of consideration, since what is not intentionally constituted has already been denied any claim to being.[19] (3) A universal theory need not actually be universally applied; it is sufficient that its applicability be universal, and this it is from the fact that nothing scientific could possibly escape its influence; to be scientific and to be constituted in reason are synonomous. Unfortunately this last answer completely begs the question,

---

17. A theme which he takes up again with great vigor in *Krisis der europäischen Wissenschaften*, cf. p. 333; cf. *Formale und transzendentale Logik*, pp. 226–35.

18. Husserl's objection to "system" in the strict (e.g. Hegelian) sense.

19. This effectively throws out the whole of Kant's *Critique of Practical Reason*, concerned as it is with God, Freedom, and Immortality, which are scarcely reducible to the phenomenal order. Incidentally, this same claim refuses a priori any criticism of phenomenology as such.

and yet it is in terms of this answer that we must try to understand Husserl's project of a universal rationalization of being.

If there be a universal science wherein is contained the justification of all particular sciences, there can be no science superior to it wherein it would find its justification;[20] that would immediately be a denial of its universality. It must, then, contain its own justification, which, according to Husserl, it can do if it constitutes the very sense of science as such. This is no more than to say that it constitutes the very sense of the most universal object of science, the sense of "being" itself.[21] Now, how is it possible to have an assurance that the very sense of being is accounted for in a science? Only if absolutely nothing which is essential to being can escape the a priori of reason, apart from which nothing can be known with absolute necessity and hence scientifically. But, if the very essence of rationality is constitution in reason, then being itself will escape the a priori of reason, if its essence is not constituted in reason. Nor does Husserl shrink from this conclusion: a universal science of being is possible, precisely because it is possible to constitute in reason the essence of being.[22]

Whatever else this may be, it is not a subjective creation of being. Rather, it is an affirmation that essence, be it the very essence of being, is inconceivable except as the object of reason and that an object of reason is inconceivable except as *constituted* in reason. The essence of being is the necessary *sense* of being, and there is no other source of necessity than reason. Kant, of course, was equally convinced that necessity could be sought only in reason and, therefore, that no science is possible except in dependence on the a priori of reason. The difference is in the conclusions that Kant and Husserl draw from the same conviction. Kant concludes therefrom that a "universal" science of being is impossible, since not all being can

20. For this reason Husserl, like Aristotle, calls this supreme science "first philosophy."

21. *Formale und transzendentale Logik,* p. 242.

22. With this, existence ceases to be a problem. Since existence adds nothing to being (cf. Kant, *Kritik der reinen Vernunft,* B 626–27), in knowing essence we know all that is to be known. If this essence exists, it is in no way changed (i.e. there is no change in its intelligibility).

be brought under the a priori of reason. But Husserl concludes therefrom that a universal science of being is possible, precisely because there simply is no essence which can escape reason. Unfortunately this affirmation does little more than define essence as that which has its source in the a priori of reason, which is but another way of identifying essence and meaning.[23]

There is, however, considerable significance in the fact that Husserl does not use the term "meaning" (Bedeutung) but rather the term "sense" (Sinn). The term may seem insignificant, but it is intended to indicate the difference between the arbitrary and the necessary. That the distinction is possible at all in a purely immanent theory of cognition is due to the fact that in this theory consciousness is conceived of as intentional. Intentionality plus necessity gives absolutely certain knowledge; and both intentionality and necessity reside in consciousness. Looked at merely as intentional, the grasp which consciousness has of an object is the object's "meaning." Looked at as not only intentional but necessary, the grasp which consciousness has of an object is the object's "sense" or essence. Thus, with perfect consistency a theory of knowledge has developed into a theory of being. To know being scientifically is to know its essence, and to know its essence is to have an intention which presents itself with absolute necessity to consciousness. Finally, to say that an intention presents itself with absolute necessity to consciousness is to say that it has been constituted in reason. It is for this reason that transcendental subjectivity is so important. It is the necessary essence which contains within itself the "laws" of intentional constitution. What is constituted in accord with these "laws" is eo ipso necessary.

There are, of course, still problems to be met. One of them is to show that the necessity which is predicated of reason is truly universal and not merely a necessity resident in the particular subject who happens to be employing the phenomenological method.[24] Another is to show that there is any necessity at all. It is all very well to identify essence and that which is constituted in consciousness with necessity: that involves no logical inconsistency. But suppose

23. Cf. Schlick, "Is there a Factual A Priori?"
24. Again, the problem of "logical" vs. "psychological" necessity.

there simply is no necessary constitution, in the sense in which Husserl understands it. He has violently rejected as an explanation any sort of psychological necessity, which is in itself hard enough to prove, in favor of the sort of objective necessity which has always been assumed to inhere in logic. Logical necessity, however, is generally recognized as formal necessity, and what Husserl wants is material and formal necessity. The question may well be asked if he has succeeded in showing anything more than formal necessity, the kind of necessity involved in perfect consistency with one's definitions. If there is rational constitution, which by definition would be necessary constitution, then the object of such constitution would be an essence. Logically speaking it would be formally correct to call such a necessarily constituted object an essence, but the whole question is whether Husserl in forty years succeeded in elaborating more than a formal logic [25] — which is but another way of asking whether Husserl advanced *as far* as Kant, to say nothing of going *beyond* Kant.

The very fact that Husserl has had such an influence on thinkers of obvious caliber, such as Scheler, Heidegger, von Hildebrand, Ricoeur, Sartre, and Merleau-Ponty, would seem to imply that phenomenology is more than an elaborate formal logic. On the other hand, neither the fact of influence nor even the general acceptability (if it is acceptable) of the method are indications that Husserl achieved this aim in the way he thought he did. It is rather remarkable that, having spoken so much about necessity, Husserl did not take the trouble to tell us what the essence of necessity is. By his own admission one can scarcely say *that* there is necessity if one does not know *what* necessity is. And yet absolutely everything depends on *necessary constitution in reason.* It would seem that the very basis for the whole "science" of philosophy is unscientific. Now, this is not to say that the whole theory is not genial; it simply makes it somewhat doubtful that the whole theory is genuinely rational. We might say that Husserl has rationalized experience, but that the price he paid was to irrationalize reason. This may very well be the greatness of Husserl, that his fundamental intuitions are not rational

25. Is the identification of "constitution" and "intuition" merely a matter of semantics?

at all — he is only rational "after the fact," somewhat as were Descartes and Spinoza.

In this connection it is significant that none of Husserl's more prominent disciples followed him in his "complete" rationalism. This has been interpreted as a fear of the sort of idealism which such rationalism involves, but it would seem that the distrust is even more fundamental. Is it even desirable to rationalize philosophy, or does not such a rationalization involve an impoverishment that the true philosopher cannot accept? What validity has the value judgment which puts rational thought above other forms of thought? Constitutive phenomenology tells us much about *essences*; does it tell us anything about *being*? According to Heidegger, Husserl is concerned exclusively with *that which is* (*das Seiende*) and not at all with being (*das Sein*), with the *true*, but not at all with *truth*. Is it worth the price one must pay? It has never been demonstrated that certainty has any supreme value, particularly if certitude requires spending forty years to perfect the method whereby it is to be obtained, only to find at the end that one's own disciples have abandoned the quest.

Still, the above criticism of phenomenology's results should not be construed as a condemnation either of the method or of the aims in their generality. There is no question that the history of philosophy from Plato on has attributed to certain conceptual analyses a value which they simply do not possess. Like Kant, Husserl has the merit of having presented conceptual analyses for what they are, without attempting an unjustified extrapolation into the nonconceptual order. To have recognized essence as something characteristic of mental conception is to Husserl's credit, even though a preoccupation with certitude blinded him to the irreducible element in all being. Still, he is not the only essentialist in the history of philosophy, nor should we ignore the contribution which essential investigations can make to thought. Alfred North Whitehead praised the scholastics for having contributed much "penetration in the handling of ideas." [26] Phenomenology has done the same. It has the added merit of having sent us back to experience without at the same time

26. Cf. *The Function of Reason* (Princeton: Princeton University Press, 1929), p. 36. The whole book is a brilliant defense of reason, but not its *deification*.

allowing us to bog down in a mere phenomenism. It is characteristic of phenomenology, no matter what its form, to claim to tell us something of what things are, and not only to remind us of how things appear to us. At the same time it warns us not to construct from appearances conclusions which the data do not justify. It is for this reason, perhaps, that the last of Husserl's published works takes on a particular importance by insisting that the proper philosophical act is one of meditation rather than of syllogistic reasoning from mental construction to mental construction.

The original title of Husserl's *Cartesian Meditations* was *An Introduction to Transcendental Phenomenology*. As an "Introduction" the book is pretty heavy going, particularly for those who are not already familiar with Husserl's thought. As a model of philosophical meditations, however, it reveals an approach to being which has proved rich in results for those who have had the courage to follow it. Husserl always considered himself a Cartesian, despite obvious differences between his thought and that of the "Father of Modern Philosophy." He saw the essence of Cartesianism in the passionate desire to justify all cognition rationally, and he saw only one means to accomplish his universal justification. Demonstrations, syllogisms, proofs were of no avail, since they could not justify themselves.[27] What is more, they necessarily involved a departure from the data of consciousness, the only data which could be "given" absolutely. All that was left was a prolonged "meditation" *on* the data of consciousness, whereby he could progressively see more clearly what they contained. Thus, philosophical knowledge represents no more than naïve consciousness, to which is added the *qualification* of necessity. As has been mentioned already, the works of Husserl contain very few of such actual meditations, but they do contain an elaborate outline of a method for making such meditations. It is as though Husserl were to say, "I cannot by demonstration compel you to accept anything I say, but if you make the same meditation I make, I am convinced you will *see* things the way I do."

Eugen Fink, one of Husserl's most faithful interpreters, explains

27. Cf. *Philosophie als strenge Wissenschaft*, p. 341.

this as a desire on Husserl's part to get people thinking phenomenologically — the rest will take care of itself. In a somewhat
disconcerting passage, Fink tells us that one cannot even understand phenomenology until one is a phenomenologist.[28] It is because Husserl is convinced of this that he is concerned throughout
his career with convincing phenomenologists that their meditations
will be rich in essential insights into every field of objectivity. Thus,
we find Husserl as a professor assigning to his students various phenomenological investigations, much as a scientist might assign to his
students laboratory experiments. Many of the results were gathered
in the *Jahrbuch für Philosophie und phänomenologische Forschung,*
edited by Husserl from 1915 to 1930. A complete reading of its contributions, particularly those by Edith Stein, Moritz Geiger, Alexan-
der Pfänder, and Max Scheler, will transport the reader into a phenomenological atmosphere of prolonged meditation on experience,
in the broad sense of that term. The purpose of these meditations
is to examine minutely experiences (which can be presumed to be
common) and to discover all these experiences can tell us, without, however, presuming to deduce from the experiences what is
not contained in them. In one way or another, each meditation
seeks to tell us not what things do but what things are. Each is,
as it were, an appeal to make the meditation along with the author
and thus convince oneself of the results.

Because these particular meditations are presented for those who
are presumed not only to be familiar with phenomenological techniques but also willing to apply them, scarcely any appeal is made
to method; it is simply employed. On the other hand, in his own
writings, with rare exceptions, Husserl is constantly appealing to
the method, constantly explaining what he thinks may not yet
be clear, constantly developing its implications in an attempt to
meet all the modifications which the matter in question may involve.
Besides this, however, one has the suspicion that Husserl's constant
insistence on method has another motive too. When one reads the
articles of the *Jahrbuch,* the impression is inescapable that even
Husserl's closest disciples are not in full agreement with him, par-

28. "Die phänomenologische Philosophie Ed. Husserls," pp. 368–70.

ticularly on the utter radicality of the reductions, the ideality of the objectivities with which they are concerned, and the universality of intentional constitution. And so, the *Cartesian Meditations* can be looked upon as an affirmation by Husserl that he has taken back nothing of what he had formerly said, plus a renewed act of faith in the capacity of the phenomenological method in the strict sense to take care of everything.

For this reason it is particularly interesting to follow through the thought of the *Cartesian Meditations,* published toward the end of Husserl's career and containing a sort of manifesto indicating what the founder of the movement considered genuine phenomenology to be. In these "meditations" we find familiar themes repeated; but we also find the most complete and systematic treatment of the phenomenological ideal which Husserl's writings afford. It is truly an "introduction to phenomenology" in the sense that it is concerned exclusively with *what* phenomenology is and *how* its results are to be achieved — not at all with what its actual analyses reveal. As has been pointed out before, phenomenology, as Husserl understands it, stands or falls with the adequacy of an analysis of transcendental subjectivity as the a priori source of all objectivity. Thus, the *Cartesian Meditations* lose little time in getting to the heart of things; if all true knowledge is ultimately a knowledge of transcendental subjectivity, then the task is to show how all is contained in subjectivity. To those who are aware of the Husserlian problematic, however, it may seem strange that so little is said specifically therein on the problem of temporality. Quite obviously temporality has its application in the discussion of genetic constitution, objective and subjective, but the specific problems of temporality are scarcely discussed.

This fact we may attribute to something of an historical accident. The lectures, of which the *Meditations* are a development, were delivered in 1929, approximately three years prior to the period of intense application to the problem of temporality. The broad outlines of an analysis may have already been present in Husserl's thought, but apparently he preferred merely to indicate the problem and leave a more detailed discussion to a later date. Furthermore, if we look at the large group of manuscripts from 1932 to 1936 which treat of this problem we can understand a certain hesitation in treating, in quasi-popular lectures, of matter which even seven years later remains substantially obscure.

Apart from this one point, however, by analysing briefly the contents of the *Meditations,* we can get a good over-all picture of transcendental phenomenology as developed by Husserl himself.[29]

FIRST MEDITATION: A PHILOSOPHICAL EXAMINATION OF CONSCIENCE. The first Meditation, which is rather brief, seeks to conduct the reader immediately to an examination of the transcendental *ego.* Thus, Husserl wastes no time in giving concrete form to the Cartesian ideal of an absolute science oriented toward the totality of being. In order to do this he deliberately presupposes that the ideal of such an absolute total science is valid; he seeks an absolute certitude, without, for the moment, asking whether it will involve certitude of any thing but itself. This certitude is the *cogito*; the question is, can it serve as the foundation for a truly scientific philosophy? Only, says Husserl, by rejecting the Cartesian prejudice that such a universal science must be mathematical can the ideal be realized — nothing can be presupposed, only the ideal itself, not even the possibility of its realization.[30] Actually, however, he is presupposing the possibility of a realization, since only thus, he is convinced, can all other sciences be legitimated, and they *must* be legitimated. The ideal of a universal science is contained in the very significance of the scientific effort; it is as though he were to say, "mankind cannot get along without science, but without a scientific *philosophy* there can be no science of any kind." What-

29. With the publication of *Die Krisis der europäischen Wissenschaften und die transzendentale Phänomenologie* in 1954, Husserl's approach to the problem of history has been brought to the attention of scholars; in it, however, Husserl seeks to solve the problem on the basis of principles already developed. In the first volume of *Erste Philosophie (1923/24),* published under the auspices of the Husserl Archives in Louvain, there are some interesting elaborations on these same principles, but there is nothing fundamentally new.

30. As a matter of fact, Husserl begins with *two* presuppositions: one, that the idea of an absolute foundation for *all* sciences is legitimate, precisely as an idea; the other, that the science which would supply this foundation is to be called philosophy.

ever be the science in question, it can be guaranteed only by an absolute criterion; but the only possible absolute criterion is that an object be absolutely *given* to consciousness.[31] Thus, the true scientist can be satisfied only with an absolute *givenness*. Where is that to be found?

A scientific judgment cannot be completely justified unless all its presuppositions are completely evident, and this they are only if they are given to consciousness *in* themselves and not *through* something else. Such an absolute evidence must exclude any possibility of doubt, and that is possible only if they are given the same degree of indubitability as the *cogito* itself.[32] This indubitability, however, is not to be derived *from* the *cogito*; it is to be found *in* the *cogito* or not at all.[33] Convinced, then, that absolute certitude can be found in the *cogito*, Husserl introduced the epoche, as a means of eliminating all that is not part and parcel of the *cogito*, and he introduced the *reductions*, as a progressive inclusion of objectivities *in* the *cogito*.

Now, if we look at the *cogito* not as the individual act of consciousness but as the whole complexus of conscious acts, we have the subjectivity as such,[34] which becomes that wherein alone objectivity is contained. The fact that this subjectivity has not been attained until all existence (*Dasein*) has been eliminated takes away nothing, since what has been eliminated is precisely nothing; what has been left is being in its true sense. What is left is the reality (*Wirklichkeit*) of the *cogito*, i.e., the pure life of consciousness, which is subjectivity, wherein alone objectivity *is* absolutely. "I am" is given,[35] and with this is given a world. Because the world is given as "over against" the *ego*, the world transcends the *ego*, and because this is true the *ego* is transcendental. Thus, at one and the same time

31. This in direct contradiction to the prevalent positivism of his day.

32. Here Husserl rejoins Descartes, whose criterion of certitude is: "Am I as sure of this conclusion as I am of the *cogito*?" See *Discourse on Method*, p. 33.

33. There is a hint here of Husserl's whole procedure. He has unceremoniously rejected one member of the disjunction (nor does he later justify the rejection, as he has promised), i.e. that the certitude is not to be found. It must be found, therefore, and only in the *cogito* is it to be found.

34. A peculiarly logical subject.

35. What Husserl actually recognizes as given is "there is consciousness."

there is given a *pure* subject, absolutely certain because involving only the *cogito,* and a *transcendental* subject, because it contains a world which is given as absolutely as is the subject.

SECOND MEDITATION: THE TRANSCENDENTAL REALM OF EXPERIENCE. The conclusion reached in the first Meditation is that the *ego* is the first absolute certainty, present to consciousness in the very evidence of the *cogito.* No more is needed, according to Husserl, to show that there is an absolute certitude anterior to all *objective* knowledge. This, however, is still not enough for the purpose he has in mind; the *ego* thus grasped is but an empty certitude. If no more than the *ego* is certain, then no advance has been made. The question must be asked: how fruitful is this absolute certitude of the *ego?* Is anything added by the fact that this *ego* is transcendental? The *Cartesian Meditations* were written precisely to answer this question, and each Meditation is intended as a step toward showing what is contained in this subjective certitude. Thus, the second Meditation aims at clarifying the whole field of *transcendental* experience, whose content is no different from that of *naïve* experience, but which is given the guarantee of apodictic certainty, because its evidence is exactly the same as that of the *cogito.* It has always been admitted that one can be mistaken with regard to *what* one experiences but not with regard to the *fact* that one is experiencing.[36] If, then, there is some way by which the totality of objective references contained in experience can be given the same evidence as there is for the *ego,* the *what* of experience is so tied to the *that* that one cannot be right about the one and wrong about the other. Thus, there is a complete field of experience, coextensive with the naïve field, which cannot be subjected to doubt. All that is needed is to ensure that the objective reference of experience be as immanent as the experience itself.

If, for example, one perceives a tree, there can be reason to

36. It might, of course, be objected that one can be certain of experiencing (in the broad sense) without knowing what kind of experience it is — perception, imagination, memory, anticipation, etc. Husserl, however, feels that he has already made sufficiently clear in his earlier works how one "experience" is to be distinguished from another. The purpose of the *Logische Untersuchungen* was precisely to make this clear.

doubt that there *exists* a tree corresponding to this perception, or that the perception faithfully represents something outside the percipient. There cannot, according to Husserl, be any doubt that one is *perceiving* nor that one is perceiving a *tree*. If one is content to know *that* one is perceiving and to know *what* one is perceiving (the what being *given* as evidently as the perceiving), then an absolute science of objectivity is possible, of the kind of objectivity inseparable from the act of experience. For such a science nothing need be consulted except experience itself. Experience contains within itself all that need be known about it, and this it reveals to the inquiring gaze armed with the proper technique for deciphering it. *Mutatis mutandis,* this is true for any experience whatever.

The question, of course, might be asked about error: Is it to be eliminated as simply as all this? If not, is it not necessary to begin by criticizing the very procedure whereby it is to be avoided? Husserl's answer is a peculiar one. He admits the possibility of error even in a transcendental analysis of experience but he denies that this is the place to institute a critique. This sort of thing is new, and one should first become habituated to the novelty of it before looking for the weaknesses in it.[37] The critical stage comes after one is accustomed to transcendental analysis and is to be effectuated in a "constitutive critique" which recognizes phenomenology as a hundred percent subjective philosophy — a philosophy which must be fully exploited, even at the risk of a complete solipsism. Husserl is sanguine that all danger of solipsism will be eliminated with his theory of intersubjectivity, but that must wait till the end; for the present we must go on *as though* this were the purest solipsism.[38] Unfortunately, *Die Krisis der europäischen Wissenschaften* was writ-

37. As with the validity of the scientific ideal, Husserl is here demanding a sort of act of faith. Unfortunately the critique which is ultimately offered will be looked on as valid only by those who have taken the present steps. Thus, phenomenology can legitimately be criticized only by a phenomenologist, who is not likely to do so.

38. It is this willingness to postpone solutions which gives the *Cartesianische Meditationen* their "systematic" character. It is also what makes them unsatisfactory, since a "system" which does not terminate satisfactorily is unsatisfactory as a whole. Cf. the criticisms of Roman Ingarden, given as an appendix to the *Cartesianische Meditationen*, particularly pp. 211–12.

ten *as though* this problem had already been solved, thus to a certain extent vitiating many of its otherwise brilliant analyses.[39]

How, then, is such a position to be developed? The phenomenologist must exploit that element of the Cartesian *cogito* which Descartes himself let lie fallow — the *cogitationes*. They are what the new science *knows*. Genuine reflection, we have seen, is infallible; and reflection on the *ego* is necessarily reflection on its experiences; the *ego* is its experiences. The world to which experiences are naïvely assumed to be related *may* be an illusion; the experiences themselves as *relations* to a world are absolutely indubitable. Now, simple experience says of itself neither that the object to which it is related exists nor that it does not exist; only reflection says one or the other. If this is so, then one can *choose* the kind of reflection which makes the world purely phenomenal — that is, neither existing nor not existing, simply *appearing*. It comes down to a difference in interest; one can be interested in the world or in experience of the world. If one chooses the first one can go wrong; if one chooses the second, one cannot. Husserl has chosen the second, because his main *interest* is in not going wrong — in achieving a *science* at any cost.[40] Thus, phenomenology deliberately limits its interest to finding out what the experience of the world is.

Every experience is a relation to objectivity in a world of objectivity. Now, every relation must have two terms — that is the essence of relation. Experience, however, is not *merely* a relation of two terms; it is a synthesis of multiple modes of appearing, the term of which is *that which* appears. Still, what appears is not distinct from the appearance in the sense of being *other than* its appearance; rather it *is* the synthesis of modes of appearing, constituted in experience. It is for this reason that a strict science of what appears is possible; it is a science so long as it seeks *only* to tell us what experiences are — in themselves and in their objective reference — and that is all Husserl *wants* to know.[41] He will know

39. It is for this reason that attention to this work has been confined almost exclusively to the author's few remarks at the end of Chap. 8 (see *infra*, pp. 161–62).

40. Husserl is dissatisfied with Kant's *Critique of Pure Reason*, but it is the only part of Kant's *Critique* to which he accords any philosophical value at all.

41. By a sort of tautology he can call this knowing *everything*, since what can-

experience as a unity of appearances and as a constant identity of that which appears (both of which are *given* in experience itself). Both unity and identity are intentional, which is but another way of saying that they are immanent in experience.

Now, if we continue to consider experience in the broad sense presented in *Formal and Transcendental Logic*,[42] we can say that an examination of both the actual and the possible modes of consciousness reveals to us the a priori laws of experience. By the same token, without quitting the field of pure immanence, we can say that a constant identity [43] running through all modes of consciousness constitutes objectivity. In a certain sense this may seem arbitrary, but it is what Husserl *means* by objectivity, and if the only objectivity in which he is interested is the kind of objectivity he *means,* that is certainly his privilege. Even such an identity, however, is characterized by a succession in consciousness, since the aspects which are synthesized cannot be simultaneously present. Therein consists the interior temporality of consciousness through which every synthesis (and experience in the full sense *is* synthesis) is temporalized. Thus, if experience is necessarily temporalized, the objectivity to which it is related is correspondingly temporalized. Subjective temporality, then, is revealed in the constant "flow" of experience; and objective temporality is revealed in the successive synthesis wherein objective identity is constituted.

At this point we are faced with the philosophical paradox, which Plato saw so clearly, of an identity which is constantly changing (moving) without losing its identity. This is possible, says Husserl, only where the identity in question is *ideal*. This is the synthetic ideal unity which defines objectivity. Of objectivity in any other sense there simply could be no scientific knowledge. Such an ideal identity is neither the *abstraction* of a common denominator in experience nor the consciousness of a constant relation to an exterior identity; it is the constancy of the synthesis operated by conscious-

not be known is, by his definition, *nothing.* See *Formale und transzendentale Logik,* pp. 207–208.

42. *Erfahrung und Urteil* presents an analysis of experience in this same sense.

43. It is from this "constant identity" that Husserl derives his "laws" of intentional constitution; though it is not easy to see that this means an absolute justification of these "laws."

ness itself. The act wherein an object is constituted as identical is the synthesis of the various modes according to which the object *is* and *can be* given. It is the consciousness of identity which constitutes objectivity. Whether one sees objective identity as determining consciousness or identity of consciousness as determining objectivity, the result is, for all practical purposes, the same. For Husserl, however, the difference lies in the assurance given in the one and the other points of view.

It is important that this constitutive consciousness of identity should be the synthesis which *effects* identity. It is essential to synthesis that it conform to the fundamental form of all synthesis, which is the interior consciousness of time: "The basic form of this universal synthesis, which makes possible all other synthesis of consciousness, is the interior consciousness of time which embraces all." [44] The synthesis wherein time is constituted is the first synthesis, without which no other synthesis is possible, which is but another way of saying that no matter what the synthesis, in it is constituted a temporally qualified object. It is the temporal *cogito* which demands that its correlate be temporal, so that we can say: to be given as phenomenal is to be given as temporal. What is more, not only is the temporal form of synthesis fundamental, it is the form of synthesis which is most proper to reflection, since the objects of reflection belong essentially to a constant intentional "flow." This is doubly true, since any intuition of essence must take into account not only the objective aspects which are *actually* present to consciousness but also the "horizons" of aspects which are *virtually* present thereto. Because an object is always more than what is actually present to consciousness, the essence of an object cannot be constituted except in a *successive* actualization of aspects — to which must be added the sum total of the horizons constituted by the whole of experience, which dominate the form of total experience which is the "interior life." [45] Since the essential correlate of the *cogito,* which is the

44. *Cartesianische Meditationen,* p. 81; cf. *Phänomenologie des inneren Zeitbewusstseins,* p. 412.
45. This is really a profound intuition, though not necessarily new: that every experience of mine is what it is because colored by the sum total of my experiences. No one else can experience exactly as I do, because no one else has my history.

cogitatum, cannot be isolated from the total "flow," horizons, too, must be analyzed, if objectivity is to be grasped adequately.

The remainder of the Second Meditation consists in an explanation of how the naïvely intended object is to act as a "transcendental guide" in the definitive analysis of objectivity. This we have already seen, and it suffices here to point out that the explanation is intended as a preparation for a complete rationalization of naïve experience, with its naïvely accepted object.

THIRD MEDITATION: THE ROLE OF REASON. Up to this point phenomenology has been concerned with inculcating a new attitude with regard to the objects with which consciousness finds itself presented. The elimination of the sort of transcendence which makes for doubt has resulted in two discoveries: (1) the *transcendental* subjectivity as the first absolute datum; and (2) the inclusion of all objectivity — actual or potential, by virtue of intentionality — in this transcendental subjectivity. Still, it is one thing to state that being and truth, evidence and certitude, can be discovered only in transcendental subjectivity, and another, to be sure *when* they are or are not present. There must be no question that in consciousness not only truth but also error is to be found, even after the elimination of transcendence; otherwise the epoche could suffice to guarantee truth, and "philosophy" would be very simple indeed. If this is so, then transcendental subjectivity will not be the foundation of all objectively valid cognition unless it contains within itself the guarantee that the being it intends is true being. How are we to know that we are in possession of true being, and without going outside consciousness itself for an answer? In the concrete this means: What is there intrinsic to experience which can tell me that experience is objectively valid?

The answer to this question has been hinted at in the Second Meditation: consciousness has its own "laws," its necessary a priori structures. If we understand objectivity as Husserl has explained it, a constitution in correspondence with these a priori laws will necessarily be valid, since it will fulfill the very definition of objectivity. If no other objectivity is logically possible, then, by definition, the objectivity in question is valid.[46] The only problem, then, is whether the laws of consciousness (of its constitution) can be discovered. According to Husserl, it is sufficient to submit the operations of consciousness to a phenomenological investigation in order to discover the necessary laws whereby they are regulated; and this is sufficient to determine the validity of the object therein constituted. The whole point is to discover in the acts of consciousness a necessity which is not merely psychological. This Husserl is convinced he has found in the noetico-noematic structure of every act of consciousness. To all intents and purposes such a necessity is no more than logical, but it is the whole theme of the *Formal and Transcendental Logic* that the very fact of constitution [47] transforms logical necessity into ontological necessity.[48] For Husserl, as for Kant, the element of necessity is the key to the whole problem of science. In the *Cartesian Meditations* he attempts to develop a theory of necessity, whereby phenomenology becomes a pure theory of reason.

Phenomenology is not a *science* of being merely because it is phenomenology; it must be of a special kind, concerned with *true* being, with apodictic evidence, with absolute knowledge. This necessarily involves the capacity of determining with certitude when consciousness is in possession of being in the true sense. All of which means that it must be a phenomenology of *reason,* since by definition reason is the "faculty" which has absolute being for its object. If, then, phenomenology is to be a strict science it must pass through three steps: (1) the reduction of all being to a correlate of consciousness, since phenomenality is a *condition* of absoluteness; (2) the reduction of phenomenal being to the state of being given-in-itself, since only when being is thus evident can there be question of

46. This is an attempt on Husserl's part to meet Hume on his own ground — at best a risky thing to do.

47. Like so many thinkers, Husserl has imperceptibly transformed an hypothesis into a fact. Intentional constitution is an hypothesis which answers many perplexing questions; to call it a *fact* is somewhat premature.

48. Hegel's *Logic* attempts a similar transformation. We must remember, however, that it is preceded by a phenomenology, wherein the dialectic of desire has broken through the reflexive circle. It would seem that the reflexive circle must be broken through, if being is to be anything but merely logical.

knowledge in the strict sense; (3) the reduction of all knowledge to a systematized whole, since only when all actual and potential intentions have been methodically exploited and systematically ordered is there a *science* of being. These stages, however, are not merely successive; they are interdependent. The reduction to phenomenality has significance only in function of an absolute grasp of being; and an absolute grasp of being is impossible except in a framework which embraces *all* knowledge, at least potentially — and this framework is the ensemble of a priori *laws* which govern knowledge as such, since necessity means law.

Science is not to present consciousness with new objects; rather, it is to *guarantee* the objects which consciousness already has. As we have seen in the *Formal and Transcendental Logic,* science can guarantee only in constituting, since without constitution there simply are no objects. If, then, reason is to be the ultimate guarantee of science, there must be a mode of constitution proper to reason, something more than a mere grasp of objectivity, which can be nonscientific. This, unfortunately, is a little too simple; Husserl needs only to say that a priori necessary constitution is what he *means* by reason. Granted that there *is* such a necessary constitution, the problem is half solved. Add to this the capacity of being sure *when* there is necessary constitution, and the problem is completely solved. But, *is there* such a necessary constitution; and if there is, can we be sure of it? The whole of transcendental phenomenology stands or falls with the answers to these two questions. One cannot escape the conviction that phenomenology begins with very unphenomenological *insights,* which it is then *determined* to make phenomenological. Thus, the will plays as important a part as the intellect. In this connection it is significant that the greatness of most phenomenological contributions is measured by the pre-phenomenological insights rather than by the phenomenological "justification" of these insights.[49]

To get back to Husserl's own conviction: the supreme guarantee of truth is the assurance that a judgment has been commanded by

49. The appeal, for example, which we find in the ethics of Max Scheler or of Dietrich von Hildebrand owes more to its Augustinian foundation than to its phenomenological elaboration.

reason; such a judgment cannot be erroneous — if it were it would not be a judgment of reason. This, however, seems to leave open the possibility that any judgment whatever can be erroneous, since to discover that it is erroneous is simply to discover that it is *not* a judgment of reason, not what would be the *true* judgment in the case. Is there any way of being sure that a particular judgment is a judgment of reason and therefore that it is infallible, that it is no longer subject to correction? Husserl is convinced that it is possible to determine the *laws* of rational constitution and thus to be sure when a judgment corresponds with these laws. That, in fact, he conceives as his contribution to the science of phenomenology: not the infallible judgments about being — except in rare instances — but the determination of the laws which make infallible judgments possible. In the abstract this would not commit Husserl to any concrete judgment whatever, since the *ideal* laws would still be valid even if no concrete judgment would fully correspond. In the concrete, however, an ideal without application would scarcely justify forty years of intense effort; and Husserl was convinced that he had accomplished more than an inapplicable ideal.

It is the function of reason, so to speak, to "re-create" reality; and Husserl is satisfied that he has discovered the laws which make such a "re-creation" absolutely certain in its results. Certitude, of course, demands an assurance of permanence, and no factual judgment simply as such contains within itself this assurance. Permanence can be secured only by inclusion in the sum total, which by its totality is endowed with permanence. Such a totality is the pure transcendental subjectivity, the ultimate guarantee of reason itself — not in the sense that there has to be a guarantee that reason is infallible in its operation, which it is by definition, but in the sense that we must be sure that it is reason which is in operation. This assurance is to be found only in the complete grasp of that whole which is subjectivity. Thus, we are returned once more to the transcendental subjectivity. This is not, however, merely the return to what is central in a theory; it is a step forward in the sense that it is an attempt to determine what, in the concrete, a transcendental subject involves.

FOURTH MEDITATION: THE UNIVERSAL A PRIORI IN THE CONCRETE. There is little need here to devote much space to the Fourth Cartesian Meditation, since it has already been drawn on extensively in the explanation of genetic constitution of subjectivity. Still, we must look at this all-important Meditation once more if we are to understand Husserl's conviction that he has avoided a merely logical relationship of subjectivity and objectivity, beyond which the first three Meditations clearly do not go. It is unquestionably not sufficient that knowledge be absolute, if that does not also mean that it is knowledge *of something*; i.e., that it is genuinely objective. It should be clear, too, that the *need* of a universal synthesis of evidence, in order that knowledge itself be guaranteed, is no guarantee that there is in the concrete such a universal synthesis. It is not enough to say that reason is the "faculty of necessity" — since that is merely an essential definition — somehow it must be shown that effectively *there is* a "faculty of necessity," whose operation is determinable.[50] Properly speaking, however, Husserl never does show this; rather, he describes the operation of subjectivity in the concrete, hoping that his readers will *see* in this the answer to all transcendental problems. That he should, in a purely immanent theory, confine himself to this is understandable. That he has, in so confining himself, successfully broken out of the logical circle is at least questionable. Still, it is at the same time unquestionable that, given some other means of breaking out of this circle, Husserl's insights can be very helpful in analyzing what reason does present.

It should be remarked, however, that there is a distinction in Husserl's thought between "concrete" and "factual." He is concerned with showing what a concrete subject *must* be; he is not at all concerned with analyzing any factual subject, unless it be as an *example* of the essential constitution of any subject as such. The problem is posed, as soon as the attempt is made to get away from the static subjective analyses of *Ideas I*. Subjectivity is genuine only as a con-

---

50. It seems safe to say that only rationalists become skeptics, since only those who *want* complete rationality can be disappointed. Because of such a fundamental desire, Sartre finds the world "absurd." Husserl was, fortunately, not as "rationalistic" as he claimed to be.

stant *flow* of experiences; but analysis would be an illusion, if this same subjectivity were not endowed with a *determinable* identity and constancy. How reconcile permanence, without which subjectivity would be an illusion, with the progressive constitution of objectivity to which subjective constitution must correspond? In effect, this is the same as asking: How can there be history, since that of which there is a history must both remain the same and constantly change? A simple solution might be to posit some sort of Aristotelian *substance,* but of this Husserl will have nothing; it is a conclusion *from* evidence, not contained *in* the evidence itself.[51] What the evidence does present is a sum total of objects, and hence of objective references, which is constantly moving. One can make a purely logical synthesis by merely correlating the two streams — any *noematic* structure bespeaks a corresponding *noetic* structure — but to do this could be to remain immersed in the abstraction Husserl is trying to escape.

The only way out seems to be to objectify the *ego* in some way. To do so in the way one objectifies "things" would, of course, involve a patent contradiction, but there must at least be an objective *grasp* of the *ego* — it *has,* as a subject, *cogitationes.* That such an *ego* be not substance, it is necessary that change be seen as the *flow* of *cogitationes* and that identity be seen as the *continuity* of this same flow.[52] Here once more, it is the theory of constitution which gives a hint for the solution: not only actualities but also possibilities are what they are as constituted. Thus, not everything is possible to every subject; possibility itself is conditioned by the subject whose possibility it is. No one denies that there is an *order* in possibilities, which is to say that some possibilities can be actualized only *after* others have been actualized. This order, according to Husserl, provides the evidence in which the subject is grasped. There is a "sedimentation" of constituted objectivities, and in this are constituted the "habits"

51. Like Berkeley and Hume, Husserl sees no possibility of "experiencing" substance, even if experience be taken in the broadest possible sense.

52. There is, of course, nothing new here. The difference is that the Platonic-Aristotelian tradition has concluded from the *same data* that only a substantial subject can make sense.

whereby the subject is determined as *this* subject; i.e., as subject with these possibilities. Self-constitution, then, involves permanence and identity because it is continuous.[53] Thus, too, the world ceases to be abstraction; it is not just any world, but the world of this concrete subject. To speak of a world at all is to speak of a constant objective identity, and to this corresponds a constant subjective identity, which is the concrete *ego*. The "horizons" of possibility are what they are because they are the "horizons" of this subject.

Quite obviously, if essential intuitions mean anything, they mean that a concrete subject must correspond with what has been recognized as the essence of subjectivity. Now, just as it is not necessary to analyze all experience in order to *see* the essence of experience, neither is it necessary to examine all the evidence for subjectivity in order to *see* the essence of subjectivity. Any world whatever, as the objective correlate of experience, reveals the essential structural laws of the *ego* as such, which is inseparably bound up with the essence of experience. To put it another way, in my consciousness of my own world I am, as a subject, constantly given to myself in the evidence of my experiences. Knowing *what* experience is I know what the *ego must* be; knowing experience as essentially a continuous flow I know *how* the *ego* must develop. Knowledge of the concrete is determined by knowledge of the *laws* governing essence — *flow* is constant change, but it is determined by *law*. Thus, when Husserl speaks of "active genesis" or original constitution and of "passive genesis" or motivation he is speaking of determinable laws of subjective development. Unlike the common conception of the law, however, Husserl's conception never implies *causality*; rather, an observable constancy of operation makes possible an intuition of an a priori necessity in operation — since the operation is intentional and not physical, causality is simply meaningless. One advantage which Husserl feels he has gained by this approach is that it permits him to reintroduce many psychological problems, such as the genesis of common representations (e.g., of "thing," space, time, etc.), without reintroducing the factual analyses upon which so much of experimental psychology is based. He is not unaware, however, that this

---

53. Sleep, amnesia, etc. pose, of course, a serious difficulty for this continuity.

advantage entails a disadvantage: if it is the essence of experience to belong to a flow, then what becomes of a *first* experience? All experiences can be related according to a noncausal law, but there is no law for the first experience — does this invalidate the whole law?[54] To put all this into a social or historical framework does away with the need of *assigning* a beginning, but it does not solve the fundamental problem.

When Descartes had pushed law as far back as it would go he felt constrained to take refuge in the *divina veracitas*. This Husserl looks upon as a sort of rational cowardice; he himself will resolutely appeal only to human reason itself. In the long run, however, this is but an *act of faith* in reason; there is no ultimate verification of reason itself. There may well be some connection between this and Husserl's almost frantic appeals to his method. One would say that he deliberately avoids concrete applications of the method; it is for him to reveal how cognition must work, it is for others to work out the details. On the other hand, such a theory has to be more than a methodology; it is a philosophy of being precisely because it is a transcendental theory of cognition; it is concerned with *laws* which determine not only cognition but also its object. It is, however, precisely as a philosophy that its ultimate basis is choice and not reason. It matters little that this choice happens to be called "intuition." Lest this choice be deemed purely subjective, however, Husserl feels constrained to show that the very universality which objectivity requires is not an abstract but a concrete universality. The laws of cognition (and hence of being) are not merely a description of how Husserl's mind works; they must govern the operation of all subjectivity and they must terminate in objectivities which are necessarily valid for all subjects. This attempt at concrete universalization, however, must form the matter of a new chapter.

54. This, of course, is the fundamental dilemma of all rationalism. Beginnings can never be strictly rationalized, yet all subsequent rationalization is rendered suspect by the initial failure.

8

THE OTHER EXPLAINED INTENTIONALLY

FIFTH MEDITATION: Up to the present Husserl has been content to explain the universally a priori laws of cognition and hence of being on the level of a reflection wherein the subject requires no other equipment than its own subjectivity. The laws of *all* subjectivity are discoverable in the transcendental *ego*,[1] since an intuition of their validity establishes them as essential and hence infallible. Still, even while examining the problematic of the *Logical Investigations* one could have seen that a purely solipsistic explanation of intentional constitution would ultimately prove inadequate. In that early work, the starting point of the investigations is to be found in an analysis of discourse. If there are "empty" or "unfulfilled" intentions, the reason is that concepts have somehow been communicated through discourse, and these concepts have not been critically examined. Now, if communication constitutes a phenomenological problem, the solution cannot be confined to a solipsistic justification of the concepts which figure in discourse. If there is communication at all, no matter what its explanation be, there must be a plurality of subjects who communicate. Incidentally, if a phenomenologist writes a book, he does so in order to communicate his own convictions to others, nor can he as a consistent phenomenologist be satisfied with the naïve assumption that there are other subjects who will understand what he seeks to communicate.

If, then, we assume with Husserl that there can be no explanation of being in any form outside of intentional constitution, the problem becomes infinitely more complicated, just at the moment when a solution seems imminent. The constitution of objectivity has been

---

1. No possible subject can be *essentially* different from the *ego* discovered in an essential intuition.

explained; the concomitant constitution of one's own subjectivity has been explained too. What has not been explained is the presence (or even possibility) of other subjects, which, if they are to be significant, must be constituted, but which would seem to resist any attempt at a constitutive explanation. The *essential* laws of subjective constitution have already been discovered; if a subject is constituted in any other way, either its constitution is not valid and the result is zero (at least scientifically), or the laws which have been discovered are not essential. Both of these conclusions are inadmissible: the first because it would destroy the universality of phenomenological science; the second because it would destroy the scientific character of universal phenomenology.

If we reject both conclusions, then we must face the dilemma of a constitution which is not objective, since its term is a subject; nor can this constitution be subjective, since, as we have been made to believe up to the present, subjective constitution is self-constitution, whereas what we are seeking is some sort of constitution of one subject by *another*. We have, it is true, been told in the Fourth Meditation of an objective constitution of a subject, but this had to be subsequent to its subjective constitution. We have not been told of an objective constitution whose direct form is a subject. The self is constituted in and with its experiences, but since I cannot constitute another's experiences, how can I constitute another's subjectivity? And, if I cannot do this, how can another *be for me*? Is there a third kind of constitution, which is neither objective nor subjective, or is there a synthesis of objective and subjective constitution wherein is constituted an object, which is at the same time a subject? The Fourth Meditation contains a hint as to the answer in its insistence that the constituted subject can be concretized by being objectified — by reflection we can grasp our own subjectivity as an object. It remains to find a means of grasping some element of the objective world as a subject.

Although, as we said before, Husserl prefers to lay down the rules of intentional constitution and leave the details of concrete application to others, this is one concrete application which he cannot bypass. His own notion of universally valid objectivity makes it imperative that his universal subject be not abstract but concrete; and a concrete universal subject means nothing if it does not mean a concrete multiplicity of subjects. Now, if there are many subjects, many conclusions follow which have not yet been so much as suggested: (1) Each subject must be self constituted, else it can have no significance in a phenomenological framework. (2) Each subject must be constituted as such (either individually or collectively) in each other subject, or the result will be a completely monadological universe, where communication is impossible. (3) The constitution of the other must correspond to the other's self-constitution, else it will be invalid; and my constitution of self must correspond to others' constitution of me,[2] else I will be myself and not myself. (4) Each must constitute a world of objectivity which is in some sense identical with the world constituted by the others, or there will be no common ground for communication. (5) The world which each one constitutes must be a world comprising oneself and others, else the unity of the world will be destroyed, as Sartre has destroyed it by making the self ultimately the "néant."

Husserl was certainly not unaware of all these problems involved in his theory of intentional constitution. It is for this reason that he spent so much time during the last years of his life trying to evolve a consistent theory of intersubjective constitution. It is doubtful whether he himself was convinced that the theory as he was able to evolve it answered all the questions which can be legitimately asked, but there is no doubt that he saw no reason in the intersubjective problematic for abandoning the completely constitutive explanation of all being for which he had opted. Having once and for all rejected any possibility of a causal explanation of cognition, the only consistent thing to do was to reject with equal vigor any causal explanation of intersubjective communication. Thus, though in many places Husserl gives evidence of having conceived this theory of intersubjectivity as an additional guarantee for the validity of subjective constitution, it is difficult to see how the theory as actually evolved does any more than explain how the fundamental theory of consti-

2. This, obviously, admits of degrees; no one need know me as I know myself. Still, one constitution cannot contradict another.

tution can be extended to the presence of other subjects in the cognitive field, without thereby adding anything to the already developed theory. The theory of intersubjectivity is, as it were, a particular application of intentional constitution, an application which could not be avoided, as were most other applications, since the central concept of objective validity demands an objectivity recognized as binding on *all possible* subjects; and the very admission that other subjects are possible demands that the theory account for the constitution of such subjects — even if only as possible.[3] Thus, it is impossible to escape the impression that the numerous pages consecrated by Husserl, in both his published and unpublished works, to intersubjective constitution add no explanation whatever to the problem of objectivity.[4] Rather, intersubjective constitution is but an extension of the theory of objective constitution, concerned with an object which is constituted both as an object and as a subject. It is difficult to see how it could be more than this without entering into the existential problematic, which Husserl never effectively does. It is for this reason that we have devoted a separate chapter to the Fifth Cartesian Meditation, since it seems to be conceived as a particular application of what has been developed in the first four Meditations.

Understood in this way the problem is traceable to a certain paradox inherent in the very notion of intentional constitution, particularly when viewed as a constitution of the *ego,* as it is in the Fourth Meditation. Such an *ego* must be at one and the same time *constitutive* and *constituted.* We ourselves can be *in the world* only to the extent that we are for ourselves *objects* in the world, since the world has been defined as the totality of objects for a subject. Now it is clear that the self-constitution described in the Fourth Meditation is not the constitution of an object; it is the progressive constitution of a "pure" subject, in and through a series of objective references to an

3. Admittedly, it is difficult to conceive what possibility can mean in that which is *merely* possible. Can there be a possibility without reference to actuality? Nicolai Hartmann has instituted a detailed critique of "logical possibility" in *Möglichkeit und Wirklichkeit* (2nd ed.; Berlin: de Gruyter, 1949).

4. The best known are the Fifth Cartesian Meditation and *Ideen II.* In the latter Husserl is concerned with laying the groundwork for a genuine essential psychology.

objectively constituted world. On the other hand, it is clear both from the Fourth Meditation and from the psychological studies of *Ideas II* that the transcendental *ego* both *can* and *should* be objectified. The important thing to remember is that when the *ego* is objectified, its constitution does not enjoy the same priority as does subjective constitution; it is preceded by the world in general, constituted as a sum total of objectivity. By a sort of paradox it is also preceded, according to Husserl, by the constitution of the other subject, as the first example of object which is also subject.[5] If we could look upon this as a recognition on the part of Husserl that a subject is not fully constituted as subject except in a community of subjects, we might consider the whole thing a modification of his general theory. Thus, it could be said that the other subject is genuinely *given with* the proper subject, precisely because it is essential to a subject that it not be given in isolation. This seems to be the position of phenomenologists like Scheler and Heidegger, but it is too Hegelian in tone to have been acceptable to Husserl.[6]

Now, the problem of the other, known as a subject, is not confined to phenomenology. Every philosophy must recognize among its field of objects one object which is like none of the others; it is presented not only as known by the knower but also as knowing the knower.[7] The difficulty is that to be subject means to have experiences; to be experienced as subject is to be experienced as having experiences. Somehow, then, the experiences of others must form part of my intentional life, without at the same time being my experiences. Consequently, Husserl is obliged to find an intentional category comprising some sort of experience of others' experiences. This one can do somehow, he says, by "empathy" (*Einfühlung*).[8] In empathy

5. Cf. *Ideen II*, Beilage X, pp. 324–25, Beilage XII, p. 351; Mss C 11 V, p. 8, B I 9 VI, pp. 31–32.

6. There is a hint in *Krisis der europäischen Wissenschaften*, No. 54, that Husserl was leaning toward some such explanation.

7. More than anyone else, perhaps, Hegel has exploited this recognition in a series of dialectics leading up to consciousness of self; cf. *Phänomenologie des Geistes*, ed. Lasson (Hamburg: Meiner, 1948), pp. 133–71. J.-P. Sartre has pushed the same thing to a pathological extreme; cf. *L'être et le néant*, pp. 310–68, 431–503; *Huis clos*.

8. Unfortunately this notion seems to have been contrived in order to fill a need.

Husserl finds the key to a constituted world which will be objectively valid for all subjects — actual or possible. What he has done, however, is to realize that such a solution demands a kind of intentional experience which has for its object the experiences of others. Since such an intentional experience is necessary, he postulates it and calls it "empathy." Still, this procedure is not as arbitrary as it might seem: Husserl does not pretend in his explanation that empathy is a known phenomenon, whose essence he has intuited; rather it is a sort of tentative explanation of what he is convinced will be ultimately explained intentionally — though the explanation may have to come from more detailed investigations.[9] As Eugen Fink puts it, Husserl has no intention of interpreting empathy but merely of using it as an "explicitation of the reduction,"[10] whereby the first contact with other subjects on the naïve level is raised to the transcendental level. Once more the naïve object — which is here a subject — acts as "transcendental guide" for the phenomenological investigation.

To get back to the argument of the Fifth Meditation, we can, simply by placing ourselves at the point to which the Fourth Meditation has brought us, distinguish three elements absolutely *given* to pure consciousness. They are: (1) my animated body (*Leib*), infallibly perceived as a material object; (2) my soul (*Seele*), as the psychological subject of objectifying operations; (3) the body of the other (*Körper*), not considered as either animated or inanimate, but simply as an object resembling my own body.[11] The point,

Much, of course, has been said about it in contemporary psychology and aesthetic theory, but from them Husserl has borrowed little more than the name. As for a phenomenological analysis of empathy, it seems to be confined to saying what it *must* be if it is to fulfill the function for which Husserl needs it.

9. Cf. *Philosophie als strenge Wissenschaft*, p. 322, n. 1.

10. "Die phänomenologische Philosophie Ed. Husserls," p. 368. The concept has been put to good use in the realm of aesthetics by Theodor Lipps, *Aesthetik*, I (Leipzig: Voss, 1914), pp. 96–223, and by Max Scheler, *Wesen und Formen der Sympathie* (5th ed.; Frankfurt am Main: Schulte-Bulmke, 1948), pp. 259–65, in the realm of psychology.

11. Husserl has, in fact, said little or nothing of these three *objects* in the Fourth Meditation. He is presupposing them as belonging to the stage reached there; they are explained in *Ideen II*.

then, is to show that, by virtue of the principle of "association," [12] there is given with these objects something else whose indubitability is the same as theirs. In order to show this, it is necessary, in accord with the already established phenomenological procedure, to analyze not only the given objects but also their manner of being given. If the proper subject, which is unquestionably *given* in any experience, is objectified, it is given in another way. All that is now needed is that this other mode of givenness should involve (not by causal inference) other subjects.

It is possible, by a sort of abstraction, to separate from the sum total of constituted nature a part which has sense for me and for me alone. This is my (animated) body (*Leib*), the only real object in the world which is not simply a body (*Körper*). Thus, the experience of one's own body is unique in the whole field of experience, a fact which is, of course, recognized by all philosophers. The body is given immediately as animated by a soul, and by the same token the soul is immediately given in the same evidence.[13] Herein, then, the *ego* can, so to speak, constitute itself as a "body–soul" composite, which is the psycho-physical *ego*. As such it is a transcendental subject, and, since it has been objectively constituted, it is an objective subject. Now, just as the subjective grasp of the subject is at the same time an objective grasp of the world, constituted in the subject, so the world is contained by "association" in the objective grasp of the transcendental subject. Only on this "secondary" level of subjectivity, where the subject is grasped as an object, is it possible to distinguish that which is proper to the subject from that which is "foreign" — impossible on the level of the *pure* transcendental *ego,* since there all objectivity is equally objectivity constituted in the *ego*. On the *secondary* level, however, where the individual *ego* is distinguished from the transcendental *ego* as such, objectivities can be distinguished as constituted in this and/or that subject. And

12. It will be seen that this principle of association has been imperceptibly modified. It is not so much the calling up of a constituted objectivity through its connection with another, as it is the original but not direct constitution of an independent objectivity, the evidence for which is contained in the evidence of other objectivities.

13. Since the epoche and reductions are still operative, the "soul" is not given as substantial, merely as a center of reference for "psychic" operations.

here, for the first time, it is possible to grasp what is experience for others. Thus, by distinguishing within the generality of the transcendental *ego* between what is foreign and what is proper, one has an intuition of one's own individual subjectivity, which when grasped in the sort of constant identity which characterizes an object becomes a *personal* subject.

Once the individuation of the proper personal *ego* within the pure transcendental *ego* has been accomplished, the *possibility* of other individual subjects has been seen, as particular participations of the universally valid idea of subjectivity. And, just as phenomenological interpretation of the world is a constitution of the evidence in which the world is given, so too a phenomenological interpretation of the other will be a constitution of the evidence in which the other is given, or, it will be constitution of a world in which there are other subjects. Thus, the evidence of self as an individual will be the same evidence in which other individuals are given. The world is first given as the objective correlate, so to speak, of a transcendental *we,* but the very first differentiation of subjects within this *we* gives both self and others. In this, however, there is a certain convergence of evidence: the proper subject is first given vaguely as subject in general and then objectified as individual; the other is first given as a sort of object in general and then subjectified as individual. What is primarily given, then, is the world and with it pure transcendental subjectivity. With this, by a sort of association, is given the differentiation of multiple subjects, which is to say that the *meaning* of multiple subjects has been constituted.

Still, since the other represented in this way has no other determination than that of being a subject and of not being myself,[14] it is as yet a subject demanding positive determination. The first determination is purely objective: the body (*Körper*) of the other is perceived as an object. By an associative transfer, however, it is grasped as an animated body (*Leib*). It is by its *behavior* that the other's body is perceived as similar to one's own body. And so, although the other is presented as an intentional modification of my own field of

14. Remarkably similar to the beginning of the Fichtean dialectic of *ego* and *non-ego.*

perception, of my own *ego,* it is at the same time presented as an *ego,* that is, having its own correlative world. It is possible to take the simple determinations of "here" and "there" as corporeal characteristics and to realize through them a distinction between *this body here* and *that body there,* which is ultimately a distinction between two subjects. I can comprehend the other as a subject having the experiences I *would* have if I were *there.*[15] This, of course, demands that the subject have already had a series of experiences in which the same object is recognized as the same from "here" and from "there."

Once another subject is recognized, however vaguely, as having experiences similar to one's own of a world which is also one's own world, the step to a recognition of the world as object of a *common* constitution is not a long one, though what a "common constitution" can mean must remain vague. What is more, this raises a further difficulty with regard to the constitution of the other subjectivity. As subjectivity it must certainly be self-constituted, and as individual subject it must be objectively constituted. Now, for me ꞏ ꞏ ꞏⁿstituted as "there," whereas for itself it is constituted as which is to say, it is not constituted in both cases as absontical, since "here" and "there" are modes of corporeity to distinguish bodies and, hence, subjects. Husserl's answer rporeal nature is commonly constituted with two distinct ꞏs whereby there are two subjects. This may seem insignifi-t it is enough to indicate that common constitution stops at n generality; particularization involves a differentiation ced by individual subjects. It may be that two subjects ex-ꞏe things (or *some* things) in exactly the same way, but there vay of *knowing* that this agreement is anything but general. the world is commonly constituted, but the result is a com-world with different modalities, so that the one world is for ent subjects both the same and different. The sameness is dis-ꞏable in the a priori *laws* of intentional constitution, which are

There is a peculiar oversimplification here, based on the conviction that the intuition of subjectivity so gives the essence of experience that a multiplica-of subjects cannot significantly modify this "essence."

determined on the level of pure transcendental subjectivity, prior to any distinction of multiple subjects. All of which makes one wonder if other subjects are genuinely *given* or whether what is given is merely that any other possible subject must correspond to the essence of subjectivity.

The theory of intersubjectivity, however, does permit Husserl to approach a subjective community not too far removed from the one Hegel presents in his *Phenomenology of Spirit*. This, perhaps, is the real significance of the theory. In self-constitution it is first the pure transcendental subject which is constituted as the correlative of all objectivity. Only thereafter is the subject constituted as a recognizable object. With the other subject the process is precisely the reverse — first objectivity, then subjectivity. And, just as there is a sort of correspondence in the constitution of the self and of the other as individual subjects, so there is a correspondence between the subjective and the intersubjective constitution of the pure transcendental subjectivity. Had Husserl been able to develop this last point more completely and more consistently he might have attained to a concrete community of consciousness, whose history would be a *total* history, because a history of "Spirit," as it is for Hegel.

On the objective side this theory does introduce an important distinction which appears only late in Husserl's writings. The concrete individual subject, as we have seen, is limited by the world therein constituted. This world Husserl calls *Umwelt,* corresponding to the individual *personal* subject. Besides this, it is now possible to recognize a *personality* of a higher order, a *social* unity, having as its correspondent a "community" world, which Husserl calls the *Kulturwelt.*[16] In this, then, is discovered an intersubjective a priori, which cannot contradict but can expand the subjective a priori. Though Husserl himself does not develop the theme, one can see in it the possibility of some sort of intersubjective verification of subjective insights. Were this more thoroughly developed it might silence some of the objections which continue to find Husserl's whole methodology too arbitrary.[17] Husserl himself is convinced

16. Cf. *Cartesianische Meditationen*, pp. 168–77; *Ideen II,* Nos. 50–51.

17. One can find hints of this sort of "social" development, from different points

that this intersubjective a priori excludes any arbitrariness in constitution, making it resemble a "discovery" far more than a "creation," and by the same token making it profoundly *metaphysical*.[18]

The importance of the theory, then, is not so much in the actual explanation which is given as in the realization that some sort of explanation is necessary, if transcendental phenomenology is to be a complete theory of cognition. Husserl has, in fact, remained remarkably faithful to the Kantian intuition, according to which a critique of objectivity must be essentially a critique whose aim is to establish the validity of the cognition in which objectivity is given. He also remained faithful to his own fundamental intuition, according to which cognition is not objective because it is valid, but rather is valid because objective. Now, though such an intuition demanded a new concept of objectivity evolved in the course of the transcendental analysis, it brought Husserl to the conviction that no cognition could with reason be called objective — and hence valid — unless it be a cognition effectively the same for all possible subjects. There is even a certain negative advantage to be gained from the vagueness attaching to the theory of intersubjectivity; from it we see that the most important element in the whole of transcendental phenomenology, the element of objective validity in knowledge, is not to be secured by some cut and dried technique (or techniques) which needs but good will in order to be carried out successfully. In *Ideas I* he had said that the all-embracing problem of phenomenology is intentionality,[19] but his remaining writings show that intentionality is to yield a solution to the problems of philosophy only at the cost of painstaking analysis from every side.

It would certainly be saying a great deal to say that the theory of intersubjectivity has, precisely from the point of view of theory, contributed concrete results notably superior to those already obtained on the level of *pure* transcendental subjectivity.[20] Still, if we remember that the general aim of phenomenology is to establish a method

of view, in the works of Gabriel Marcel and Maurice Merleau-Ponty; there are also hints of it in Max Scheler's remarkable *Wesen und Formen der Sympathie*, and in his sociological works.

18. *Cartesianische Meditationen*, pp. 166–68; cf. *ibid.*, pp. 108, 113.

19. *Ideen I*, p. 357.

20. Although Husserl does say it; cf. *Nachwort zu meinen Ideen*, pp. 14–15.

whereby that which was already given in consciousness prior to the application of the method should be adequately constituted — and thus verified, validated, made evident — we can recognize in this last, undeveloped theory a positive contribution in the form of an explanation of subjects as well as of objects, which is of considerable importance (as Husserl recognized in *Ideas II*), if positive psychology is to be established on a firm basis. "Other" subjects present no less a problem in any conceivable philosophy than they do in transcendental phenomenology; the only difference being that a philosophy which does not pretend to be "scientific" need not be so embarrassed at not finding a "solution." There is, nevertheless, even some justification in Husserl's contention that there is here an approach to the problematic of *existence*. In explicitating the "sense" of the other, which is already contained implicitly in the very concept of an objectivity which must be equally valid for all possible subjects, the theory of intersubjectivity recognizes that the other must be a "real" subject, if objectivity itself is to have any "sense" at all. Science, after all, can have no recognizable validity if its contents are verifiable only for one subject, even though that subject be convinced that it is the representative of subjectivity as such. If nothing else, it should be possible to show how knowledge could be communicable to others, on the mere supposition that there are others. Further, if the "science" of philosophy is to be the task of a community of scholars imbued with the same ideal and employing the same method, as we read in *Philosophy as Rigorous Science*, then this community of scholars must be more than a vague generalization.

It might, of course, be objected that Husserl has maneuvered himself into an untenable position by his insistence that philosophy be nothing less than a strict science, but that is a criticism which applies to the ideal, not to the consistency with which Husserl has tried to realize the ideal. Like every other philosopher, Husserl was a child of his times, and his times would be satisfied with nothing less than scientific verifiability for every proposition which is to be recognized as meaningful.[21] In Husserl, then, we see a heroic effort to re-establish metaphysics according to the canons set up by science.

21. Cf. *Philosophie als strenge Wissenschaft*, pp. 340–41.

It may well be doubted that he was wholly successful; it is indisputable that his researches have opened up new vistas of possibility, which have been and are being exploited by philosophers whose ultimate orientations are extremely diverse. It is precisely Husserl's faithfulness to an original ideal, expressed in the consistent effort to explain all of philosophy in terms of the phenomenal analysis which has provided the initiative for a new approach to being, which will strive to avoid mere verbal analysis and to grasp reality in the way it is present to consciousness in itself and not through symbols of itself.

Husserl himself would be the last to say that he had evolved during his career a complete philosophy, or even to say that his method has been completely formulated. More than once he expressed dissatisfaction with the formulation of that method. Of two things, however, he never ceased to be convinced: first of all, that philosophy as he conceived it could develop only in accord with the scientific ideal he had conceived from the beginning; and secondly, that no development which in any way contradicted the *essential laws* of intentional constitution, of which he would recognize no doubt, could possibly be admitted as genuinely philosophical. Modifications which spring from a deeper penetration into original intuitions could be admitted — and the theory of intersubjectivity he sees in this light — but changes which would imply that the original intuitions might not be essential could not be admitted. Within Husserl's own writings phenomenology undergoes considerable development, but it is always a rectilinear development, all of it implied in the first of all phenomenological intuitions, which is that wherein consciousness is seen as essentially "intentional" in its operation. If one is compelled to read not only all Husserl's published works but also all his manuscripts, the constant "return to beginnings" can prove extremely annoying; it is unquestionably repetitious, and it leaves precisely the most burning questions unanswered, but it bears eloquent testimony to his heroic efforts to make of phenomenology an instrument of precision for the resolution of perennial philosophical problems. For the actual fruitfulness of this method we cannot look to Husserl's own works; we must look to those who have, to a greater or less extent, drawn much of their inspiration from Husserl.

* * *

In one sense it is true to say that *The Crisis of European Sciences,* the last of Husserl's works,[22] only one third of which was published during his lifetime,[23] adds nothing doctrinal to what has already been presented in his major published works. In another sense, however, it does add something new, in that it situates historically and describes phenomenologically the "rationalism" for which Husserl had been pleading since 1900. In it the theme of *Philosophy as Rigorous Science* is renewed, but it is presented in a more consciously historical — or, at least, "teleological" — framework.[24] The forms of rationalism, from Plato to Logical Positivism, have varied considerably, though the ideal, according to Husserl, has remained substantially the same. What he attempts to show in this "last will and testament" is that forms of rationalism have succeeded — and superseded — each other down through the ages, and that particular forms have proved, in the light of those which succeed them, to be inadequate.[25] Phenomenology, then, is an historic form of rationalism. It supersedes all others, precisely because it has been

22. For an excellent summary and critique of the *Krisis,* cf. Aron Gurwitsch, "The Last Work of Edmund Husserl," *Philosophy and Phenomenological Research,* XVI, 3 (March, 1956), XVII, 3 (March, 1957).

23. The first Part was published in *Philosophia,* I (Prague, 1936).

24. This is a teleology proper to consciousness and conscious-being. An analysis of the act of consciousness shows that all its elements are oriented toward a goal, which is knowledge (cf. Ms. F I 17, pp. 154–55). The fundamental principle in the teleology of consciousness is intentionality, which is a tendency to give oneself an *object,* in the full sense of the term (cf. *Formale und transzendentale Logik,* p. 232). During the period which saw the writing of *Krisis,* Husserl sees an "historical" teleology in philosophy itself: "The entire development of philosophy as a preparatory stage for science" (*Brief an den VIII. internationalen Kongress der Philosophie in Prag,* Sept., 1934, p. 13). It is the only way one can speak of a "sense" of history in Husserl's thought.

25. Cf. Gurwitsch, *art. cit.,* II (1957), p. 397. It is characteristic of Husserl that he is better at criticizing the defects of historical positions than he is at evaluating their positive contributions.

able to rationalize our *experience* of the world. Thus, the whole of history can be interpreted as a teleological process aiming at the ultimate rationality of transcendental phenomenology.[26] No new elements of that rationality are here introduced, but it is situated as a sort of final stage in the process of safeguarding the primacy of rationality in man's historical destiny.[27] To transform the ideal of rationality in the light of modern scientific advances has proved a necessity, but the greatest tragedy for Western culture would be to interpret the transformation of the ideal as an abandonment of the ideal. As Gurwitsch says so well in summary: "Surrender to the anti-rationalistic and anti-intellectualistic tendencies, a surrender urged upon us from many quarters, is nothing short of self-betrayal of Western man and betrayal of the teleological destiny and idea of man at large. This destiny is none other than the autonomy of reason which actualizes itself in a historical process: viz., through the historical transformations of the idea of rationalism."[28]

Thus, the *Crisis* does not serve as a modification of Husserl's fundamental position. Rather, it confirms that fundamental position and, by situating it "historically" in the process toward ultimate rationality, marks the transition to those developments in phenomenology which another world of experience renders possible. In this last sense Husserl has in the *Crisis* given the "green light" to developments which, in his earlier days, he might well have considered infidelities to the ideal of transcendental phenomenology.

---

26. In "Die Ursprung der Geometrie," p. 220, Husserl gives a definition of history which leaves it in the sphere of immanence, in the sphere of "essences" and not in that of "existence." He says: "History, as we understand it, is no other than the vital movement of a formation and a sedimentation of sense, the one *with* and *in* the other." This, of course, supposes the intersubjective *ego* as a sort of concrete universal spirit, a notion which is not too comprehensible in the framework of a theory of *transcendental* intersubjectivity.

27. Husserl does not feel that philosophy has reached its goal with him, but rather that he has contributed the point of view which will enable it to reach that goal: much remains to be done, but it can be done only in a framework of transcendental phenomenology, which framework has already been outlined.

28. Gurwitsch, *art. cit.*, II, p. 396.

APPENDICES

QUESTIONING PHENOMENOLOGY

THERE SEEM TO BE at least three ways in which one can speak of phenomenology today. Assuming that the phenomenological movement is somehow identifiable, we can designate it as that contemporary philosophical movement which has Edmund Husserl as its central and still dominating figure. Only by narrowing down the field to at least this extent can we avoid calling phenomenologist every philosopher whose point of departure has been immediate experience and whose method has involved an analysis of this experience. Such an extension of the term would have to include Plato and Aristotle, Descartes and Bacon, Hegel and Nietzsche, to mention but a few. Having, then, narrowed down the field in the way just mentioned, we can classify phenomenologists in terms of their relation to Husserl's phenomenology during his later years — to his transcendental phenomenology. It is thus that we can conveniently distinguish three groups (with, of course, as many variations as there are individuals in each group). If we take the extreme transcendental idealism of Husserl, with its insistence on the universality of the reduction and its refusal to accord validity to what has not been intentionally constituted in transcendental subjectivity, we have no group, we have only Edmund Husserl himself in splendid isolation, as Herbert Spiegelberg says.[1] If, however, we take a certain faithfulness to the "constitutive intuition" of Husserl as a criterion, we

Entitled "Questioning the Phenomenologists," an earlier version of this Appendix appeared in *The Journal of Philosophy*, Vol. LVIII, No. 21 (October 12, 1961), 633–40.

1. Herbert Spiegelberg, *The Phenomenological Movement* (The Hague: Nijhoff, 1960), I, p. xxviii: "While it is true that Husserl is the founder and remains the central figure of the Movement he is also its most radical representative and that not only in the sense that he tried to go to the roots, but that he kept digging deeper and deeper, often undermining his own earlier results; he was always the most extreme member of his Movement and hence became increasingly the loneliest of them all."

have hit on a distinguishable position, which would include such proponents of phenomenology in America as Aron Gurwitsch, Dorion Cairns, Herbert Spiegelberg, and Richard Zaner. A second position, perhaps more readily identifiable, would be that of those who draw their inspiration from the Husserl of the *Logische Untersuchungen*. It would include the members of the original Göttingen and Munich circles, the collaborators of Husserl's *Jahrbuch für Philosophie und phänomenologische Forschung*, and most of those who specifically call themselves phenomenologists today. A third group would include all those whom Herbert Spiegelberg includes in his monumental survey, or at least all those who employ phenomenology as "an intuitive method for obtaining insights into essential structures."[2]

There are many reasons why it is difficult to criticize phenomenology. If, for example, we were to look upon as phenomenologists all those included in Spiegelberg's book, then it would always be possible to point to one or another who escapes the particular criticism in question, and thus the critique could be said to have missed phenomenology as such.[3] If, on the other hand, we were to confine ourselves to criticizing Husserl's own thought, on the assumption that, despite seeming variations, there is a logical unity of development in that thought, the limitation would be arbitrary, unless we could prove that a phenomenology which did not follow Husserl all the way was inconsistent with itself. A justifiable point of departure, it would seem, is Spiegelberg's quasi-definition of phenomenology as "an intuitive method of attaining insights into essential structures." If this definition is acceptable it affords the advantage of a triple approach to a reasonable critique. We can ask whether such a program is not committed to certain Husserlian positions which are themselves questionable. Or we can with Moritz Schlick[4] ask whether such a program has in fact produced anything more than some inconsequential distinctions, ultimately reducible to the dis-

2. *Ibid.*, p. 11.
3. Only a phenomenology of phenomenology would provide us with a common denominator at which criticism could be aimed.
4. "Is there a Factual *A Priori*?"

tinctions one chooses to assign to terms. Finally, we might discuss the validity of calling such a program philosophy, rather than a propaedeutic to philosophy.

Even with this limitation, however, we are not completely off the hook. Phenomenology is like the Hegelian dialectic in this, that there is doubtful justification for standing off and looking at it in order to criticize it; there is some validity in the contention that one can only *do it* and see what happens. There is the added difficulty that neither the method nor its results are ordinarily presented as being definitive, with the result that any criticism must likewise be only provisional. There can be no question that, historically speaking, phenomenology has in recent times performed the important philosophical function of directing attention more seriously to experience as the only legitimate starting point of philosophizing. In approaching it, then, we ought to speak not of a "critique of phenomenology" but of certain questions which can be put to it, which should be answered if it is to justify the enthusiasm that its proponents manifest.

PHENOMENOLOGICAL "PHILOSOPHY"

Herbert Spiegelberg has said of phenomenology that its negative aspect of an "emancipation from preconceptions" is its most teachable part.[5] There can be no question that such an emancipation would constitute a considerable contribution to philosophical thinking. It is not clear, however, that thereby phenomenology becomes a philosophy or even, strictly speaking, a philosophical method. Like Hegel's phenomenology, it might be more properly designated prephilosophical. In the course of history the philosophical enterprise has manifested itself as a rational reflection on experience.[6] An analysis of experience which makes such a reflection possible might be called a preparation for philosophizing, with all the importance

---

5. Spiegelberg, *op. cit.*, II, p. 657.

6. If, of course, the testimony of history has no role in constituting the "essence" of philosophy, as Husserl would have it, then there simply is no disputing the phenomenologist's claim that phenomenology *is* philosophy or, at least, *the* philosophical method.

that implies, somewhat in the sense in which Kant admitted that his *Critique of Pure Reason* was properly only prephilosophical.

An admission such as this might well make phenomenology's "essential insight" more acceptable, too. If one wants to make an "insight into essential structures" the goal of philosophical inquiry, there is, of course, no disputing one's choice. To me, however, such a philosophy seems arbitrarily truncated. I find essential insight and conceptualization inseparable as steps toward the goal, not as final. There is a danger that finalizing this stage will make it impossible to come to terms with existence, with history, with space, time, and movement, to say nothing of God, freedom, and immortality, speaking again in the accents of Kant. There can be no question that phenomenologists *want* to avoid conceptual fixation — Husserl himself complained bitterly at being reproached for his "Scholasticism" — but there seems reason to ask, with Dilthey, if the reproach is not to an extent justified. It is all very well to speak of the dynamic, "flowing" character of the phenomenological essence, but one wonders if this is but an uneasy union of a fixed concept of essence with an equally fixed concept of "flowing."[7] If phenomenology ceases to be analytical, does it not cease to be phenomenology? But, if it does not cease to be merely analytical, does it ever really get beyond an explication of meanings? If its aim is so to clarify the universe of discourse in which philosophical discussion takes place, its endeavors are unquestionably laudable — as a preparatory stage. There may well be no understanding until we understand meanings, but this should not mean that understanding stops there. A transcendental logic, either in the Kantian or the Husserlian sense, may be necessary. Is it, however, sufficient? Is it more than a "grammar of philosophy," with the same relation to philosophy which grammar has to literature?

This, then, brings up the further question of just how phenomenological phenomenology really is. Are the insights of Scheler and von Hildebrand, Pfänder and Heidegger, Sartre and Merleau-Ponty so different because their application of the phenomenological method varies? Or do they begin with different convictions,

7. See *supra*, p. 116, n. 45.

which they then seek to support phenomenologically? This is not to say that philosophy should be an enterprise of discovery rather than of clarification — I prefer to let the phenomenologists say what philosophy *should be* — but there is at least a suspicion that a large number of phenomenologists have their convictions *before* they phenomenologize. Intuition certainly has its merits, and clearing the ground for intuition may demand some sort of phenomenological method; but, does the method as such permit us to break out of the merely analytical circle?

Philosophy as "Science"

Another set of questions concerns the "scientific" character of phenomenology. It may be that much of Husserl's isolation from other phenomenologists is traceable to his insistence that philosophy be a "rigorous science." Since, however, it was Husserl's decision that philosophy must be scientific if it is to be genuinely philosophical, which dictated for him the phenomenological method, we might ask to what extent the scientific ideal is separable from phenomenology. This, then, immediately involves the further question: can phenomenology lay claim to being scientific without being *constitutive*? Can it be constitutive phenomenology without being *transcendental* phenomenology? To me there is a fascination in the inexorable logic with which Husserl moves from the descriptive to the phenomenological to the transcendental phase in his own enterprise. There are those, of course, for whom this movement is by no means inevitable — I am thinking particularly of Heidegger and Marcel — but the price they pay would seem to be a relinquishing of the "scientific" ideal. This may be all to the good — I am inclined to think it is — but it brings with it the specter of the arbitrary intuition and attendant arbitrary descriptions. One is reminded of Husserl's intuition into the essence of philosophy itself, which succeeds in putting all oriental philosophies beyond the pale.[8] No one had more "essential insights" than Scheler, nor can anyone be more

8. See his "Philosophy and the Crisis of European Man," trans. Quentin Lauer, pp. 157–60. It is interesting, in this context, that Husserl could spend forty years "philosophizing" as though Marx (or Nietzsche) never existed!

arbitrary than he is at times. This may be due, as Spiegelberg asserts, to the lack of phenomenological rigor in his investigations,[9] but this brings us back to Schlick's objection. Perhaps phenomenology has not yet solved the dilemma of momentous uncertainties *vs.* trivial certainties. Rationalism, after all, is rooted in a value judgment or, perhaps, in an act of faith in reason, which cannot itself be rationally justified. One is tempted to suspect that phenomenology is constructing Hegel's "temple without a holy of holies."

In speaking of arbitrariness with regard to phenomenology we do well, of course, to remember that there is a certain arbitrariness in any attempt to criticize it. Criticism would seem to imply some sort of dialogue, and dialogue implies at least a common language, a medium of communication. On both sides of this issue there is a difficulty in instituting communication — at least a communication which does not demand from one side or the other concessions which are in reality surrenders. If phenomenology can be understood only from a phenomenological point of view, as Eugen Fink, one of its ablest defenders, declares,[10] one must in practice recognize its validity before questioning it. It seems, however, that another avenue is open to one who merely asks questions. Is it not justifiable to ask just how phenomenological phenomenology is, or, better still, how phenomenological it *can* be? To put the question in another way, how viable is phenomenology without extra-phenomenological appeals? Not even Husserl imagined that phenomenology could be thoroughly "presuppositionless" in the sense that one leaves behind all one's human equipment when one begins to philosophize. The approach through the *Lebenswelt* which is characteristic of his latest writings is adequate indication of this. The phenomenological process which prepares for essential intuition is not supposed to be induction, but, when one examines it closely, in many instances it appears to be a reasonable facsimile. Phenomenology also eschews deduction — a tactic which resembles throwing away one's equip-

9. Spiegelberg, *op. cit.*, I, p. 266. In this connection it might be well to recall that Husserl himself did not attribute univocal significance to the term "science." Philosophy is not the kind of science which mathematics or positive sciences are.

10. "Die phänomenologische Philosophie Ed. Husserls," pp. 368–70.

ment before entering a fight — but deduction manages to crop up in the strangest places. There is, in fact, a monumental piece of deduction involved in the whole phenomenological enterprise. The choice of the method itself is based on the contention that only thus can we make sense of experience. This contention, in turn, is rooted in the principle that experience *should* make sense — which may very well be true, but it is a principle which has not been established phenomenologically. We are back, perhaps, to the place of the value judgment in philosophical thinking, to the act of faith in reason, which is at the root of all philosophizing, as can be seen from the "historical" disquisition of Husserl's own *Crisis of European Sciences and Transcendental Phenomenology* and other writings belonging to the same period. It is significant in this connection that neither Husserl nor, to my knowledge, the other phenomenologists have noted the importance to rationalism of Descartes's *malin génie*, calling as it does for a supra-rational justification of reason itself.

PHENOMENOLOGY AND HISTORY

It is to be feared that phenomenology in general takes a somewhat cavalier attitude toward the thought of great thinkers of the past. Not all, of course, are as extreme as Husserl, who saw in past philosophies no more than a stimulus to his own thinking, sharing, as he did, Descartes' impatience with the very existence of divergent philosophies. There is no disputing, for example, the historical erudition of a Scheler or a Heidegger, nor is it without significance that Heidegger turned more and more to etymological investigations, convinced as he was that a primitive way of speaking is evidence of a primitive way of thinking, which, in turn, brings us closer to "original experience." Still, it is doubtful that phenomenology can afford to see in the thought of great thinkers authentic evidence for the way things are — contemporary phenomenology, after all, has little if any patience with Hegel's phenomenology.

Perhaps the most consistent objection raised against phenomenology is its ahistorical character. This cannot, of course, mean that its proponents do not know their history. On the other hand, it does not mean merely that phenomenologists philosophize in a *de facto* independence of the historical current of philosophical thought, preferring to go "to things themselves" rather than to history for their inspiration. Rather, it means that as an essentialist position phenomenology is necessarily ahistorical in its approach. For a philosophy of essences the past as past can have no great significance. No matter how strongly the phenomenologist disagrees with Husserl's idealist trend, it is difficult to see how one can seek "insights into essential structures" without following Husserl in his resolute abstraction from the contingency of the factual and existent. It may very well be that history itself has an "essence," which the phenomenologist can analyze, but the suspicion remains that he can only analyze thought *about* history. The door would seem to be closed to concrete history. To speak of the past is necessarily to speak of the factual and not of the essential: one can speak of what *is* without reference to existence; one cannot speak thus of what *was* — *is* need not be existential; *was* must be. This, of course, brings us back to the "scientific" character of phenomenology; and the phenomenologist who is not too much concerned with being scientific in this sense need not be too concerned with the objection. Still, if he is looking for "essential structures," it would seem that he is concerned with possibilities rather than concrete actuality.

Maurice Merleau-Ponty has said in the preface to his *Phénoménologie de la perception*[11] that the purpose of his phenomenology is to reinsert essences into existence. There can be no question either that the endeavor is laudable or that the results in Merleau-Ponty's case are brilliant. There is still a question in my mind, however, as to what that can mean in the framework of essentialist phenomenology. If it means, as it does for Hegel, that the grasp of essence is only a stage on the way to a total grasp of reality, a meaning is certainly discernible, but it is significant that for Hegel the moment of essence belongs to logic (his metaphysics) rather than to phenomenology. I find it extremely difficult to see in a "phenomenological science" a movement from the abstract to the concrete (a *process* of concretization); I see primarily a movement from the concrete

11. (Paris: Gallimard, 1945), p. i.

to the abstract, from fact to essence. In such a framework the historical may function "by way of example" (as it does for Husserl), but scarcely as integral to the very structure of reality. One can even see a certain history of individual consciousness, but scarcely a genuinely significant history of collective consciousness.

SOLIPSISM

This last brings us to an objection which has its full force only when directed against Husserl's insistence that subjective analysis must precede intersubjective.[12] Still, along with Spiegelberg, I tend to suspect the phenomenological authenticity of a position such as Marcel's which reverses this order. It is generally admitted that Husserl was unsuccessful in coming to terms with intersubjectivity and, therefore, with community. The question, however, is whether phenomenology as such is geared to face the problem. Heidegger made a vague gesture in this direction with his notion of *Mit-sein*, but no one finds that particularly satisfactory. Sartre has instituted an almost pathological phenomenological description of the experience of other subjects, which, despite its brilliance, is at best arbitrary. Scheler, Marcel, and others have sought to analyze the experience of community. In all these cases, however, it is questionable that the phenomenological method serves as other than a vehicle for spelling out the significance of convictions which are independent of the method.

With this we are brought around full circle to the first difficulty which confronted us. Is phenomenology really a method of *obtaining* insights into essential structures, or is it a method of justifying insights which precede the application of the method? The Aristotelian philosophy of essences has traditionally had to face the charge of circularity, because the class concept which it derives from a consideration of particular instances is actually a prerequisite for the recognition of particular instances as members of the class. It could seem that phenomenology's difficulty is no less. The "essences" or "essential structures" it seeks to discern seem to govern the process of discernment in such a way that the intuition in which they are

12. *Cartesian Meditations*, trans. Dorion Cairns, pp. 116–21.

grasped initiates the process in which they are described. It might, of course, be said that the function of the phenomenological method is not so much to obtain the intuition as to guarantee its validity. This, however, does not dissipate the difficulty. One might still ask what guarantees the method or, at least, what assures us that the method has been correctly applied? — at which point, it would seem, an appeal to results would be indicated. But an appeal to results would be an appeal to the intuition.

Though I am convinced that the questions which have been asked here can be legitimately asked, I do not mean to imply that the asking of them precludes the possibility of satisfactory answers. If they can convince phenomenologists of the need there is for an examination of conscience, they will have served their purpose.

THE TRANSITION TO
EXISTENTIALISM

BY A SORT OF PARADOX not at all uncommon in the history of philosophy, Husserl, the ardent champion of "scientific" philosophy, has opened up a new and rich dimension of philosophical investigation precisely for those who would "de-scientize" philosophy. For Husserl, transcendental subjectivity, the "source of all objectivity," was the key to a "strictly scientific" philosophy. For many of those who draw their inspiration from Husserl, subjectivity is more significantly the means of transcending science in a genuinely philosophical investigation.

That this has been one of the results of Husserl's lifelong efforts is by no means sheer accident. His ideal of the philosopher as "disinterested spectator" is precisely the ideal to which he himself (fortunately) never attained. His accomplishment was rather to reveal in a most striking way to contemporary thinkers that to investigate subjectivity is not necessarily to be a subjectivist, but rather, and much more importantly, to study a necessary condition of objectivity, a subjectivity which, though not "conceptualizable," is still "graspable" in all the richness of its objective reference.

In doing this, Husserl has revealed the legitimacy of a this-worldly investigation, which, though it does not deny the possibility (or even the need) of an extrapolation, still does not institute this extrapolation, convinced as it is that things themselves have a discoverable intelligibility. The fact that such a purely descriptive investigation is inadequate to the whole of reality and must be complemented by an extension — whether causal or dialectical — does not destroy the

Entitled "The Subjectivity of Objectivity," an earlier version of this Appendix appeared in *Edmund Husserl, 1859–1959*, ed. H. L. Van Breda (The Hague: Nijhoff, 1959), pp. 167–74.

legitimacy of investigation; nor is the character of the investigation altered when it is so complemented. The phenomenological procedures of Husserl have served well those who seek to go beyond him in their penetration of reality — above all, his exploitation of subjectivity has provided contemporary thinkers with a vantage point from which to view objectivity, while avoiding the Kantian dilemma of essentialism.

That a philosophy of phenomenal being need not be a phenomenalism Husserl has abundantly manifested. To be convinced that the determination to circumscribe one's philosophical investigations within the limits of what a subjective inquiry may reveal need not be prejudicial to a contact with transcendence, may be somewhat foreign to Husserl's own intentions; it is not excluded by his method. The question here is, what a this-worldly inquiry can reveal concerning being; not, what steps must be taken in order to go beyond what this being reveals of itself.

There seems little question that Kant was talking both quite intelligently (as he always did) and quite intelligibly (as he did not always do) when he insisted that being, in the sense in which he understood being, is not a predicate, in the sense in which he understood predicate; that is, to say of something that it is, is not to differentiate it conceptually from the same thing as merely possible. The story of the hundred real Thalers and the hundred possible Thalers, which has since become legend, unquestionably contains an important truth. A hundred real Thalers are no more than a hundred possible Thalers; certainly the number is no more in either case. It is also correct to say that the intelligibility of the Thalers as Thalers and of the hundred as hundred is no greater in either case. At the same time, however, it does seem necessary to say that there is a significant difference between the hundred real and the hundred possible; intelligibility and conceptualization are not co-terminous. Not only is there a difference for the one who possesses the real as opposed to the one who thinks of the possible; there is another difference, the kind of difference which anyone introduces into a discourse when he says of something that

it is, as opposed to saying of something that it is merely understandable; a difference for everyone in that universe of discourse —
not a "purely objective" difference, but a difference in the reciprocal
relation of subject and object. .

I recall during my student days hearing a professor illustrate the
nature of a genuinely metaphysical question by asking over and
over again "What does a thing do when it is?" It should be noted,
by the way, that he did not ask "What do we say of a thing when
we say that it is?" This would be to ask for the "meaning" of
being, which, because it cannot be conceptualized, is indefinable and
has no meaning. After he had asked the question often enough it
was to be expected that one of the students would ask him, "Well,
what *does* a thing do when it is?" It might also be expected that
the only answer the professor could give was to shrug his shoulders
and say, "It is." I have since wondered whether his answer would
have been equally vague if the question which had been asked was
not "What does a thing do when it is?" but "What does a man do
when he is?" Quite obviously the second question has no more
significance than the first, if a man is looked upon simply as a thing.
If, however, a man is looked upon as a man, with all that
goes to make up this complex being which a man is, then the
question takes on a genuine significance, in fact a unique significance. Nor should this question be confused with the equally significant but distinct question "What is man?" It does not ask for a
definition of man; rather it inquires the way a man is, when he is.
The way a man is cannot be the way a thing is. A man is, we might
say, speaking existentially, when and only when he *exists*. And to
say this is clearly to give an entirely different sort of answer from
the kind which could be given to any other question about man. If
one asks, for example, "What does a man do when he runs?" we
can either describe what he does or liken it to what other beings
do in the same circumstances. No other being, however, is the way
man is — not merely because man is essentially different from any
other being, but because, in existing, man does what only man
can do. To say that a man is and that a stone is, for example, is

not merely to enumerate two "things" that are; it is man who, by existing, gives significant being to things. This giving of being we can call, for lack of a better word, a "creation."

In thus giving being to the things which are, man is also providing an answer to the question "What do things do when they are?" It is possible to ask what it is for something to be — even though the answer cannot be enunciated in a proposition — because being is accessible through the one being which stands out (ex-ists) as the center of reference for all being, the one whose being is to be center of reference, to *exist*. When things are, they are, to put it somewhat crudely, related; related to each other, I suppose, but related primarily to man, who is the center of temporal being, in the sense that he is first among beings which are temporal, but, more important, in the sense that man is the source of the temporal being of those things which are. Man, we might say, is the only being who temporalizes, not merely because he is in time and is conscious of it, but because, by being, he constitutes vital time, which is history. If one may be permitted to pun, this is precisely a *creatio ex nihilo*, because it is a creation coming from the very nothingness which man himself is. Things are, of course; but integral to their being is the determination supplied by man, to whom they are related, and who, by negating, puts them into a context of limitation and determination. Without man, there is only the chaos of brute fact: it is for man to negate this chaos, thus stripping mere fact of its "massivity," giving it "a local habitation and a name." Man is, so to speak, the point at which subjectivity is introduced into the mass of brute fact. And it is through this insertion that there is a world, a realm of "sense"; and sense is the contribution of subjectivity. The world makes sense because man is in it.

We might illustrate this in the world of values. The question has always been asked and probably will always be asked whether values are objective, which is to say inherent in objects which are valued, or subjective, which is to say contributed by subjects who evaluate. As a matter of fact, it seems that an adequate answer can be given only if we recognize, not only that values are both subjective and objective, but that they would be neither if they were not both.

There is no contradiction in saying that a value is both subjective and objective; rather it is the only way in which values can be at all. Values are "created," because without subjects *to* whom they are values there would be no values, and because the very *being* of values is a *doing* of the subjects for whom they are values. To say that values are subjective is not to say that they are not objective; it is to affirm the only kind of objectivity which makes sense. Without subjectivity there can be no objectivity; there can be no objects; there can be only chaos without significance. It can be said with truth that things are beautiful in themselves, provided we understand that "in themselves" does not mean that their beauty is entirely independent of the response which they elicit or are calculated to elicit. Things are beautiful or ugly, because there is in them that which can elicit from a subject the response which we have agreed to call aesthetic. They would not be beautiful, if there were no such response to be elicited, were there not subjects who can respond. This should not be interpreted as meaning that beauty is nothing but the response itself. Rather, beauty is the meeting of the response and what is calculated to elicit the response. The fact that there can be a response is necessary in order that there be beauty in any understandable sense of that term. By the same token, then, being is neither objective nor subjective, precisely because it is both. An object *is* in eliciting a response from a subject; the subject *is* in responding to objects. The Cartesian *cogito, ergo sum*, has recently been emended to read *respondeo, ergo sum*. To that we might add *atque res sunt*; the being of both subjects and objects is contained in the response of subjects to objects — or, better, in the reciprocal response of subjects and objects.

Thus, it is not, no more than in the case of beauty, the subject which creates the being of its object; rather, the subject in being (or, if one prefers, in existing) actualizes itself as subject and at the same time actualizes objects as objects — and, incidentally as "things." To return to Kant: he was quite right in saying that things-in-themselves are unknowable, but it was not for the right reason. They are unknowable, not because the intellect is incapable of grasping them, but because there is no such thing-in-itself. In itself, we might say, there is no-thing. To be thing is to be related to subject, not to be independent. Nor is there room, on the other hand, for Fichte's equally illusory "subject-in-itself"; to be subject is to be related to objects, not to stand in splendid isolation. It is for this reason that the world of objectivity is not deformed by the contact with subjectivity. On the contrary, it is by its very contact with subjectivity that it *becomes* a world. It is the presence of subjects in the world which makes it to be a world; the subject–object relationship is a dialogue.

Obviously what has been said up to this point should not be understood merely in terms of a cognitional response to objects. That would be precisely the too-intellectualist approach. The world of being is a world capable of eliciting a variety of responses from subjects; and the being which subjects exercise is precisely the variegated being of their response to the universe in which they are, including their response to other subjects. Just as it would be nonsense to speak of a subject for whom there are no objects, so it would be nonsense to speak of objects for which there are no subjects. Nor is this merely a question of subjects' and objects' being somehow related to each other, some sort of static mutual affinity; rather it is a mutual communication of being on the part of subjects and objects. The subject is subject, not merely because it is related to objects, but because this relation is constitutive of the very objectivity of objects. Conversely, objects are not merely related to subjects; their relatedness constitutes the very subjectivity of subjects. We do not say of an object that, in addition to being, it is related to a subject; nor do we say of subjects that, in addition to being, they are related to objects. Neither *is* fully except by being related to its counterpart; each "creates" the other — and itself.

An investigation of this sort cannot, of course, say that this is what anyone who sets out to investigate being must find. There is no question here of claiming a privileged position, outside of which lies only error; rather it is a question of setting up a universe of discourse wherein one can intelligibly discuss what it is to be within the limits of that universe of discourse. The point is, however, that this is not merely an arbitrary universe, a universe of postulates; the claim is, rather, that such an inquiry provides viable insights into the universe of being in which we live — even though it does not pretend to say the last word on this universe.

Such a view is not merely arbitrary, because it goes beneath the surface of what one individual *means* by saying of something that it is or of someone that he is. It is an attempt at a genuinely onto-logical inquiry, wherein the mystery of being is, so to speak, given an opportunity to unravel itself. At various times in the history of philosophy, this inquiry has been pursued from the point of view either of the subject encompassing a universe or of a universe en-compassing all subjects. This inquiry is an attempt to synthesize the two points of view. A universe which simply encompasses individual subjects cannot be other than opaque to these individuals. An indi-vidual subject which simply encompasses the universe cannot be other than arbitrary in its view of things. What is required, it would seem, is a universe which is a universe, only because there are subjects which make it so, and individual subjects who are subjects, only because they are in a universe which conditions their very being as subjects. Nor is this a return to the subject–object dichotomy, which has long since proved itself to be the outstanding philosophi-cal dead-end street. Rather it is an attempt to see all being as neither subjective nor objective, precisely because it is both.

There is a strong tendency, even among those who reject any psychology of faculties, to see consciousness as a sort of faculty *whereby* the human subject is conscious of that which is not sub-ject, i.e., object. Might it not be better to describe consciousness as a way of being — of being conscious? From this view it would be not inaccurate to see the world as a whole of many parts, with conscious man at its center. But, it would, perhaps, be more accurate to look upon the world as a whole which is somehow conscious, precisely because one of its parts is conscious man, without whom it simply would not be a world. The world is a world because its way of being is a conscious way of being. If we can say that the whole man is conscious, even though that whereby he is conscious may be only a part of the whole, may we not say that the world is conscious, even though that whereby it is conscious is but a part?

To return to the question "What does a thing do when it is?": we might reply "When a thing is, it is conscious." If this statement needs softening we might amend it to read "To be is to share in being conscious, which is to be in the fullest sense." A world which is in this sense, could be said to be conscious of itself, because, as a world, it necessarily includes *subjects* who are conscious, and who, by their consciousness, contribute to the being of *objects* which are, merely as objects, not conscious. The being of the non-conscious, on the other hand, enriches the being of the conscious. To be, we might say, is to act, and the being of the whole is interaction — the kind of interaction which belongs to an integrated organism.

From a personalist point of view I can say: I exist because others exist; my being as subject is to be related, not only to objects, but also to other subjects — to be *with*. But, from another point of view I can say: I am because the world is, and the world is because I am. I am not swallowed up in the world; I am not de-individualized. Rather, I am the more individualized, because I am in the world — my dignity as a man, as an individual, is not distinct from my being in the world, whereby the world is precisely this world, and I am precisely this man.

Nor does this derogate from the dignity of the Creator, who stands above both the world and man in it. Rather it enhances that dignity, since it makes Him the Creator, not of puppets, but of creators. To be is to act, and to act is to create. It is, of course, not to create the way God creates; but it is to share in the creative act whereby the universe realizes the potentialities inherent in it. Through his encounter with the world man creates himself; and it is in this encounter that the world becomes a world for him — which is ultimately to say that only through man can the world have a significance.